TOURIST

Andhra Pradesh

(The Land of Art and Architecture)

SURA MAPS

An imprint of Sura Books (Pvt) Ltd.

(An ISO 9001:2000 Certified Company)

Chennai • Ernakulam • Bengalooru

Price: Rs.70.00

Tourist Guide to Andhra Pradesh

This Edition : September, 2008
Size : 1/8 Demy
Pages : 120

Price: Rs.70.00
ISBN: 81-7478-176-5

SURA MAPS

[An imprint of Sura Books (Pvt) Ltd.]

Head Office: 1620, 'J' Block, 16th Main Road, Anna Nagar,
Chennai - 600 040.
Phones: 044-26162173, 26161099.

Branches :
- XXXII/2328, New Kalavath Road, Opp. to BSNL, Near Chennoth Glass, Palarivattom, **Ernakulam - 682 025.** Phones: 0484-3205797, 2535636
- 3638/A, IVth Cross, Opp. to Malleswaram Railway Station, Gayathri Nagar, Back gate of Subramaniya Nagar, **Bengalooru - 560 021.** Phone: 080-23324950

Printed at T. Krishna Press, Chennai - 600 102 and Published by V.V.K.Subburaj for Sura Maps [An imprint of Sura Books (Pvt) Ltd.] 1620, 'J' Block, 16th Main Road, Anna Nagar, Chennai - 600 040. Phones: 26162173, 26161099. Fax: (91) 44-26162173. e-mail: enquiry@surabooks.com; website: www.surabooks.com

09 08 2000

Contents

All About Andhra Pradesh

Facts and Figures

Capital	:	**Hyderabad**
Districts	:	23
Languages	:	Telugu, Urdu and Hindi
Area	:	2,75,069 sq. km.
Population	:	7,62,10,007 (2001 census)
Sex Ratio (Male : Female)	:	1000 : 978
Literacy Rate	:	61.1%
Growth Rate	:	15%
Density (People in Sq. Km.)	:	277
Minimum Temperature	:	11.3°C during winter
Maximum Temperature	:	44.8°C during summer
Major Airports	:	Hyderabad, Vishakapatnam and Tirupati
Minor Airports	:	Warangal, Chittoor, Vijayawada and Kakinada
Major Seaports	:	Vishakapatnam and Gangavaram deep water port (Under development)
Minor Seaports	:	Kakinada, Krishnapatnam and Machilipatnam
Season :		
Summer	:	March to June
Winter	:	October to February
Tourist Season	:	November to February (varies with places)
Lok Sabha Seats	:	42
Rajya Sabha Seats	:	18
Legislative Assembly Seats	:	295
Per Capita Income	:	Rs. 33,970 (Estimate 2007-2008)

Andhra - At A Glance

Andhra, one of the southern states of India has a medley of lavish landscape, rich traditional and cultural heritage, a series of exciting events which emblazon the pages of history and a variety of scintillating stuff, to sport. The entire state with its delighting domains had been too enticing to prevent historic inventions and counter inventions which placed one or more parts of it under the reign of various dynasties in turns. The chronicles of the region project a number of emperors of the long list of dynasties who are still survived by their bravery, benevolence, passion for architecture, patronage of arts and culture and things like that. The monuments, the flowery compositions, the literary works of the poets and scholars of yore provide an exhilarating vista of the well organised life style, culture, various forms of arts, occupation, recreation etc. of the people of the past.

History of Andhra

As long back as about 230 BC the region, under the influence of Emperor Ashoka, who made peace his way of life, nourished the prevalence of Buddhism. 'Satavahanas', then usurped the remarkable region and kept it under their valuable possession until they conceded to the invading Chalukyas in the 7th century. Then in the 14th century, the Cholas, one of the three great Tamil dynasties, conquered the coveted region. Later, a series of war broke out until the vast empire of Aurangzeb permeated over Andhra in 1713.

Geographical Location

The entire state is at an interesting geographical location. The Deccan plateau forms most part of the state. The sizzling rivers of Andhra, some seasonal and some perennial, make up to over 34 in number. The ravishing rivers Krishna and Godavari not only quench the thirst of a multitude of populace, but lend fertility too, to a vast land along their long course. About 70% of the people of Andhra are engaged in agriculture and among the produce of the state are essentials like rice, maize, millets, pulses and cash crops like tobacco, groundnut, sugarcane, cotton etc.

Forest Wealth, Agriculture, Industries

The extensive forest region which contributes to about 23% of the entire land area of the state, plays a vital role in determining monsoon and the fiscal echelon of the state since it is invariably the land of high yields of teak,

eucalyptus, cashew, bamboo, softwood and other forest products. It also helps in the conservation of wildlife. It is no wonder that with its sumptuous rice production Andhra is reckoned as the '**Granary of South**'. The state is also wayward in industries. The industries of Andhra, with their state-of-the-art technologies and latest technical know-how, bring out a variety of products which go through a series of stringent scrutiny of quality assurance and quality control before running into customers. Nature has bestowed upon the state, potentially abundant regions of copper ore, manganese, mica, coal, limestone, etc. The handloom and handicraft industry has also not lost its lustre. The lacquer toys, Anakapathi articles, exclusive pottery, black metal triklets, palm products, Dharmavaram silk and Pochampalli silk sarees which have earned an indisputable repute, etc., all bear testimony to the 'sleight of hand' behind their making.

Architecture

The ancient temples and other historic monuments of all state bring to the fore the grand architecture, traditions and conventions, faith and belief, arts and culture and suchlike interests of the glorious people of the bygone days. The architecture, sculpture and the intricate construction patterns unique to several royal dynasties are reflected in various temples of the state. The ancient temple at Tirupati dedicated to Lord Venkateswara, one of the various forms of Lord Vishnu, situated on the peak of one of the marvellous mountains of a glorious range suffused with dense forests ranks first among worship centres or second at times to Roman Catholic Church, in its income by way of pecuniary offerings and votive oblations by the millions of devotees who throng the sacred dominion of the Lord, which is also called 'Ezhumalai' or 'Seven Mountains'. The 'Tirumala Tirupati Devasthanam' is responsible for the maintenance of this temple and certain others as well. There are 'Temple Tanks' in almost all the temples here, a characteristic feature of the South Indian Temples.

There are also ancient Mosques and Churches, aplenty. The capital city, Hyderabad has a deep-felt influence of Hinduism and Islamism. The state has patronised a variety of cultures and religion during different periods in history.

Arts, Crafts & Culture

The state as a whole, has a rich and varied heritage of arts and culture. Fine arts and traditional arts have been revered and treasured from a very long past. During the hierarchical era, classical art performances were coveted with passion. And the zest has been passed on generations after generations and the 'classics' are of pristine flair among even the people of today. The art forms are indeed of a wide range.

The mirror embroidery of the style practised by the tribal women Banjaras, nomenclatured "Banjara Embroidery" is another important craft. It offers possibilities for the profitable use of embroidery skills of this economically backward community in the state.

Andhra Pradesh has a place of pride in floor coverings too. Carpets of Eluru and Warangal have long been known not only within the country but also in many parts of the world. All natural-wool pile carpets produced in these places are a speciality. The artistic Durry industry evolved in and around Warangal. Durries with floral and figurative motifs have contributed significantly to exports.

"Lepakshi", the well-known temple town in Andhra Pradesh, is a repository of stone sculpture and frescoes of a high order attained during the Vijayanagar period.

'Saint Thyagaraja', an ardent devotee of Lord Sri Rama, has produced innumerable and invaluable compositions in Telugu, the regional language of the state. His compositions are of eternal reverence as they have been sung and resung over the years and form the predominant source of 'bread and butter' to a number of artistes even today. They are an indispensable part of repertoire in any musical concert. There were also other composers whose works carry perpetual value. Even today many a big name in Carnatic music belongs to Andhra. Thus the state has been repeatedly producing great personalities in different branches of Carnatic music.

When it comes to dance, Andhra has as many as nine distinct varieties unique to its culture. Each of these varieties (viz) Veeranatyam, Butta Bommalu,

Dappu, Chindu Bhagawatham, Thappetta Gullu, Lambadi, Bonalu, Dhimsa and Kuchipudi, recounts an impressive legend or a conventional belief behind its evolution. However, all of them are aimed at devotion to God and experiencing the eternal bliss.

Taking a look at the expressions, gestures and other customary movements involved in the art performances of the region, one gets a picture of the meticulous care and prudent thought that has gone into their invention or evolution. Every bit of the dance portrays one or more events or episodes from the Holy Puranas or the great epics, aptly supported by folk, traditional or classical music, coupled with pertinent, profound percussion beats and holds the audience in rapt attention.

'**Veeranatyam**' a wonderful form of dance, very famous at Draksharamam which is where Lord Siva, according to a legend, created Lord Veerabadra out of a hair from His Jata Jhuta, the Holy lock of hair on His head, brings out the outrage of Lord Siva at the humiliation meted out to Goddess Sati Devi, His divine consort, by 'Daksha' who was the father of the Goddess during Her human sojourn. This seething dance form was first rendered by Lord Veerabadra and practised by the community known as 'Veeramusti' which is supposed to be the descendent of Lord Veerabadra.

'**Butta Bommalu**' is a dance with a touch of folk charm. Hidden in the masks lavishly made out of wood-husk, straw, and cowdung are deft performers who fill the air with the charms of folk-lore. A literal translation of 'Butta Bommalu' is 'Basket Toys' and that explains the masquerading of the dancers like gigantic toys.

'**Dappu**', a percussion instrument rightly enhances the spirit of the dancers and the audience alike. It is an indispensable part of many a festival, wedding and dance.

'**Chindu Bhagawatham**' originates from the Nizamabad district. Bright colours and beautiful costumes flash as the dancers display mythological themes with meticulous movements. Musical instruments like Cymbals, Tabla and Harmonium have a vital role to play.

'**Thappetta Gullu**', a dance that showers grace with its typical folklore to please 'Varuna' the 'Rain God' and receive showers from the Heavens, is famous in Srikakulam and Vijayanagaram districts.

'**Lambadi**', the dance that must have seen most places since it is the art form of the nomads, enunciates the agrarian chores. Glossy glass beads, tiny square and circular mirrors, ornate jewellery, ivory bangles and brass ankles emblazon the costumes of the dancers.

'**Bonalu**', the folk dance which involves the knack of balancing pots on the head while performing unrestricted movements is an inspiring sight at 'Mahakali' temples. The female performers, colourfully clad, dance their way to the temple followed by men dancers with entwined Margosa leaves tied around their waists. Men lash long whips while making rhythmic movements, according to the reverberating percussion beats.

'**Dhimsa**' is a dance of the 'Hill Tribes'. This dance is performed by women clad in typical tribal costumes. Instruments like Mori, Thudumba and Dappu add music and rhythm to the delightful sylvan dance.

'**Kuchipudi**', the famous traditional dance which originated in the village of 'Kuchelapau' or 'Kuchelapuram' is an ancient classical art which can be traced back to the 3rd century BC. Since its origin this treasured art has apparently undergone quite a few modifications at the creative hands of several patrons all over the centuries and today it is presented as a dance drama with many characters. There is a unique way of introducing the characters. 'Daru' a short, introductory sequence of music and dance is first performed by the dancers to reveal their part. One of the spectacular features of this dance is that the dancers balancing a pot full of water on their heads, fix their feet on the rim of a brass plate and make awesome, intricate, movements pressing one foot down and rising the other in turns, swirling and bending all but without letting a drop of water out of the pot.

Now, Kuchipudi is being taught in many institutions and music colleges. There is a Government-run dance school proliferating the divine art among the multitude of dedicated aspirants, at the place Kuchipudi, 60 km from Vijayawada.

If the arts of Andhra are astonishing, the crafts are captivating. The crafts with a distinct lustre have been around for centuries. The ancient rulers have doted on the articles and have been the patrons, the crafts which produced them. Many of these crafts are still much in vogue today in the form of cottage industry. The crafty hands behind every creation is lucid.

The toys, dolls and puppets made out of wood decorate the shelves of many homes. Birds, animals, mythological characters, fruits, vegetables, etc., are among the wonderful creations. The puppets find use in shadow-shows in several festivals and children shows and they seem to do justice to themselves by conveying a sublime moral from mythical events, to a lot of fascinated young eyes.

'**Sculpture**', the art of giving life to lifeless rocks has reached great heights in the state since a long past. The ancient temples and palaces bear testimony to this fact. The astounding stone images are sculpted with meticulous care given to every minute detail. Sculpture and architecture has been cherished by a number of rulers of various dynasties, the evidence of which can be seen all over the state.

'**Folk Painting**' is another craft which has been handed down to generations after generations. It is believed to have originated from the divine architect Viswakarma who out of His mercy proffered the craft to the artists on Earth. The themes painted and also the forms are mostly mythological. Wall hangers carrying these paintings decorate many homes.

'**Nirmal Painting**' finds a predominant place in the series of crafts particularly in Adilabad district. This painting, generally depicts scenes from the great epics 'The Ramayana' and 'The Mahabharatha', however, birds, animals and also fictitious figures are no exceptions. The Moghuls have practiced the craft too. Moghul miniatures on Ponkiki wood are famous.

'**Bidri**', the handicraft which conflates silver on black metal

articles has been relished by great emperors. Intricate patterns of breathtaking beauty are drawn on the black articles with shiny silver. The craft had influenced the Moghul rulers to the extent that they had all articles decorated by this craft. It is still a famous and a thriving cottage industry.

'**Bronze castings**' has also been one of the specialities of the splendid crafts of Andhra. Icons of various God-forms are made to an impeccable precision and beauty. Lord Nataraja, the dancing form of Lord Siva is one of the masterpieces of this craft.

Thus the state has varied interests and rich heritage. A panoramic view of the state may baffle the onlooker with every part of it trying to make its rival null and void in every aspect of composure. Hence, tourism is a brisk activity in Andhra Pradesh.

Festivals

Andhra has no paucity of festivals. Hindu festivals like Dasara, Deepavali, Sri Rama Navami, Sri Krishna Jayanthi,

Maha Sivarathri, Vinayaka Chathurthi etc., are celebrated with a fabulous festive fervour. There are also certain festivals exclusive to certain temples and regions like the festival '*Bathkamma*' which is celebrated in 'Telangana'. Among the Muslim festivals are *Ramadan, Bakrid* and *Id-ul-Fitr* which are celebrated with much gaiety. The Christians have their share of the 'festive cake' during *Christmas, Easter* and of course the *New Year* which is in fact relished by everyone throughout the world irrespective of caste, creed, religion or nationality.

Sankaranthi and *Ugadi* are two regional festivals which bring about bountiful mirth upon people, the former in January and the latter in March or April. Sankaranthi, an agrarian Hindu festival is marked by the worship of Sun God and Ugadi marks the beginning of New Year in the Telugu aboriginal calendar.

Lumbini festival is reminiscent of Buddhism having flourished in the region in a distant past.

HOW TO REACH

BY AIR - The capital city of Hyderabad is well connected to most major Indian cities and some overseas. The Air India has flights to Kuwait, Muscat, and Sharjah. The Indian Airlines, Air Sahara, Jet Airways, Deccan Airways runs flights to all the major cities in the country. The airport is at Begumpet, 8 km north of Abids. Auto-rickshaws and taxis are available from here. Other important airports of the state include Tirupati, Vijayawada, and Vishakapatnam. BY RAIL - There are three train stations-Hyderabad or Nampally, Secunderabad and Kacheguda. Secunderabad is the main station from where one can get trains to all major towns/cities of the country. Bookings are not made at the Kacheguda station. To go to Kolkata, one must first go to Vijayawada and then get a train. BY ROAD - Of the several bus stands in Hyderabad, the main one is the Andhra Pradesh State Road Transport Corporation (APSRTC) Hyderabad/Imlibun complex at Gowliguda. The Jubilee bus stand at Secunderabad is also very busy. From these bus stands, one can find buses to all corners of the state and some important locations of neighbouring states. Most private buses have their offices at Nampally High Road. BY PORTS - Vishakapatnam is the major port of the state, while Kakinada, Machilipatnam, Bhimunipatnam, Krishnapatnam, Vadarevu and Kalingapatnam are the minor ports.

TOURISTS ATTRACTIONS

Hyderabad, the fifth largest city in the country, is the capital of Andhra Pradesh and has several prominent places in and around it. It has a Hindu-Muslim culture with a number of monuments of historical importance like Char minar, Amber Khana, Badshahi Ashurkhana, Mecca Masjid, Osman Sagar and Osmania University. The capital is in reality the twin cities of Hyderabad and Secunderabad linked together by the Hussain Sagar Lake.

The sites of historical importance include Warangal, Palampet, Vemulavada, Bhadrachalam, and Lepakshi. Andhra Pradesh is known for pilgrimages, not only for Hindus, but also for followers of other religions like Muslims, Christians and Buddhists. The state has a rich heritage of temples, mosques, churches and viharas. The state is known for the famous Sri Venkateswara temple at Tirupati, Birla Mandir at Hyderabad and Bhadra Kali temple at Warangal, Mecca Masjid at Hyderabad, the Buddhist viharas at Nagarjunasagar, and the Sai Baba Ashram at Puttaparthi. The Hindu pilgrimage sites include Tirupati, Srisailam, Basara, and Sri Kalahasti. The state was once the site of a flowering Buddhist culture. The Salivahanas, who were Buddhists by religion, followed the Satavahana dynasty. Several Buddhist stupas and viharas were built during their reign, and Buddhist centers flourished at Nagarjunakonda, Amravati, Sankara, Bhattiprolu, Guntupalli, Gantasala, Salihunda, Panigiri, Nelakondapalli and Bahvikonda.

There are waterfalls at Ethipothala, Kuntala, and Gandipet. The caves at Undavalli and Borra are also major tourist attractions. Two large and world famous dams are located at Nagarjunasagar and Nizamsagar.

Many wildlife sanctuaries can be found in the state, namely, Kawal, Sivaram, Pakhal, Pranahita, Eturnagaram, Kinnerasani, Papikonda, Nagarjunasagar, Srisailam, Pocharam, Gundlabrahmeshwaram, Shri Venkateshwara, Srilanka Malleswara, and Kaundinya. There are four bird sanctuaries in the state at Kolleru, Rollapadu, Nelapattu and Manjeera.

The state has nearly 1,000 km of coastline, with eight of its 23 districts having direct access to the sea with azure water caressing golden sands, which accounts for the presence of so many beaches. Starting from Bhimunipatnam near Vishakapatnam down to Mypad in Nellore district, the coastline of Andhra Pradesh offers unalloyed joy to the sun worshippers and sea bathers. Apart from the Ramakrishna beach, Lawson's bay and Rishikonda beach at Vishakapatnam and Bhimunipatnam beaches there are other famous beaches such as Manginapudi, near Machilipattnam, Kakinada, Chirala, Kalingapatnam and Mypad.

Hyderabad / Secunderabad

Hyderabad is the capital of Andhra Pradesh and the fifth largest city in India. This cosmopolitan city has rail and road links with Chennai-Delhi, Chennai-Calcutta and Chennai-Mumbai railway lines. It can also be reached by air. Hyderabad and Secunderabad are separated by not more than a mile in between, are rightly known as **twin cities**. The beautiful city with all its modern structures and facilities has not failed to retain its old charm. There are ancient monuments of historic importance. There are enough specimen to evince the influence of Medieval Indian, Saracenic Mughal and later the colonial English architecture.

The city also has ancient Mosques, palacial forts, magnificent palaces, placid lakes and picnic spots. The art galleries and public garden draw thousands of tourists. In Hyderabad, the Hindu, Islamic and Saracenic architecture fuse together to bring out a secular structure.

The mean temperature in summer is around 22°C while it soars up to a maximum of 43°C at times. The winter temperature hovers beween a minimum of 12°C and a maximum of 22°C.

'**Bidri**' and '**Kinkhab**', the traditional handicrafts are still cherished in Hyderabad. '*Bidri*' is the art which adorns black metal articles with silver designs which leads to striking comparisons with a dark night sky being ripped apart by sparkling streaks of lightning. The Bidri style of decorations found on Moghuls' weapons evince how much they doted on the art. *Kinkhab* is an equally intricate art which decorates silk garments with gold and silver embroidery.

Secunderabad is situated about 10 km on the east of its 'twin' city Hyderabad. The road on the bund of the beautiful Hussain Sagar lake connects the two cities. The vast parade ground, race course and polo ground signify the importance the city has enjoyed in the past. The British had one of their largest military establishments here. An observatory and the Saifabad Palace are situated on the east of Hussain Sagar lake. The Rashtrapathi Nilayam at Bolarum serves as the living quarters of the President whenever the president visits the place.

There is a number of historic monuments around the city, far and near. The famous Nehru Zoological Park here is among the largest ones in Asia.

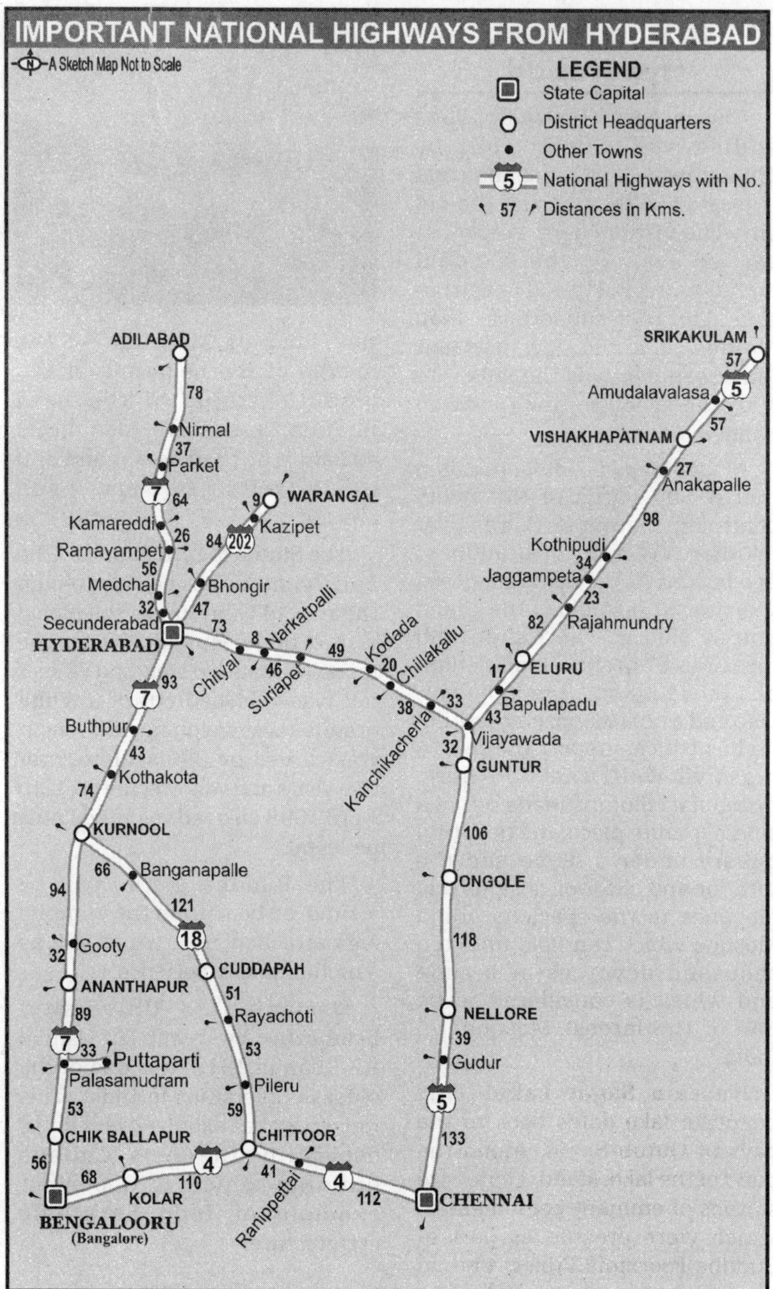
IMPORTANT NATIONAL HIGHWAYS FROM HYDERABAD
A Sketch Map Not to Scale
LEGEND
State Capital
District Headquarters
Other Towns
National Highways with No.
Distances in Kms.
ADILABAD
Nirmal
Parket
Kamareddi
Ramayampet
Medchal
Secunderabad
HYDERABAD
WARANGAL
Kazipet
Bhongir
Chityal
Narkatpalli
Suriapet
Kodada
Chillakallu
Kanchikacherla
Vijayawada
GUNTUR
Bapulapadu
ELURU
Rajahmundry
Jaggampeta
Kothipudi
Anakapalle
VISHAKHAPATNAM
Amudalavalasa
SRIKAKULAM
Buthpur
Kothakota
KURNOOL
Banganapalle
Gooty
ANANTHAPUR
CUDDAPAH
Rayachoti
Pileru
Puttaparti
Palasamudram
CHIK BALLAPUR
CHITTOOR
KOLAR
Ranippettai
BENGALOORU
(Bangalore)
ONGOLE
NELLORE
Gudur
CHENNAI

In and Around Hyderabad

Charminar: This marvellous edifice was built in 1591 by Muhammad Quli Qutub Shah and is located in the heart of the old city. The visitors here simply get carried away by the splendid architecture and grand construction. The roof supports a small Mosque. '*Charminar*', with its four famous minarets is the favourite subject of many portraits and wall hangers.

Mecca Masjid: Not longer than just a 100 yards of the ever-charming charminar there is yet another structure of grandness and beauty. As the name suggests, this Masjid resembles the grand one at Mecca. The sacred hall measures 67 m and 54 m in length and breadth and 23 m in height. One and a quarter dozen beautiful arches which support the roof, a massive wall, the two huge octagonal columns made out of a single granite piece, the beautiful gallery under a dome and the interior and exterior designs add elegance to the spacious grand Mosque which can hold upto ten thousand devotees at a time and which is considered to be one of the largest Mosques in India.

Hussain Sagar Lake: This beautiful lake dates back to the days of Qutub Shahi. Along the bund of the lake, stand 33 life-size statues of eminent personalities, which were erected as part of Buddha Poorxima Project and on

the 'Rock of Gibraltar' in the middle of the beautiful lake, a gigantic statue of the Lord Buddha, a massive monolithic structure of 18 m height and 350 tonne weight has also been erected.

The Statue of Lord Buddha : The Buddha statue has been placed on the rock of Gibraltar in the placid waters of the Hussain Sagar. The monolithic statue standing 72 feet tall was chiselled out of a white granite rock, weighing 450 tons.It was carved by 200 sculptors for two years and was erected on 12th April 1992 on a red coloured Lotus pedestal.

The Buddha statue can be visited by boat from the Lumbini Park attached to it, which will be a memorable experience.

Osmania University: Established by Nawab Mir Osman Ali Khan in 1918, it is one of the oldest universities in India. This university has exquisite buildings, especially the Arts College building which is a perfect example of Indo Saracenic architecture.

In 2001, this esteemed university was honored with five-star grade by the National Accreditation and Assessment Council (NAAC). The university has been working for over nine decades with the notion of 'Thamasoma Jyothirgamaya' (Lead me from darkness into light) and contributing to the academic, social and economic development of India.

Another fact about this university is that it is one amongst the largest universities, having no less than 3, 00,000 students in its campus and numerous affiliated colleges. Funded and managed by the government, Osmania is a non-profit university.

KBR National Park: Located in the Jubilee Hills in Hyderabad, this Park (earlier known as Chiran Palace Gardens) is the genuine wilderness area with over 100 species of birds, 20 species of reptiles and 15 species of butterflies. Jubilee Hills lies northwest of Hyderabad city center and about eight km from it.

Established in 1994 to safeguard the biodiversity and richness of the area, the park is named after late Kasu Brahmananda Reddy, the former Chief Minister of Andhra Pradesh. Covering an area of 156.30 hectares this picturesque park is unique in its own way. The tremendous diversity of birds includes species like drongos, partridges. The micro faunas are even more significant. This Park is right at the top of the most significant catchments in the heart of the city and is the main source of the Banjara and Hussain Sagar Lakes. The Park will be open from 06.00 to 08.00 hrs. and 16.00 to 18.00 hrs.

Entry Fee : Adult : Rs.20/-
Child : Rs.10/-

The Mrugavani National park: This park covering an area of 3.60 sq. km (700 acres) was established in October, 1994 near Himayatsagar lake at a distance of 25 kms from Hyderabad.

This park has over 600 plant species including herbs, shrubs, climbers and trees like Teak, Rosewood, Sandalwood, Neem, Bamboo etc are found here. The fauna comprises of wild boar, jackals, foxes, porcupines, Black naped Hare, Monitor lizards, Forest Cat, Civet Cat, Mongoose, Cheetal or Spotted deer, Sambar etc and a wide variety of reptiles including Pythons, Cobra, Rat Snakes, Russell's Viper, Monitor Lizard etc. Over 100 species of birds have been identified in the park including Peacocks, Quails, Warblers, Babblers, Flower Peckers, Partridges, Lapwings, Ducks and Curlews.

The climate is pleasant for most parts of the year. The park has a high view point and a watch tower to watch the animals at close quarters. Snake shows are conducted for tourists. The park has a well-stocked library, an Environmental Education Center with an auditorium and a museum with wildlife exhibits. There are tents, dormitories and cottages available for stay in the park.

Mahavir Harina Vanasthali National Park : Located at 15 km from Hyderabad, this National Park is a popular destination amongst the lovers of wildlife. Situated in Vanasthalipuram, the park was established in 1975 and named after 'Lord Mahavira', to commemorate the 2500th birth anniversary of the prodigy. Once the hunting ground of the 'Nizams', this park was later developed into a full-fledged sanctuary by the Government of India.

During monsoons, Vanasthali National Park appears mesmerizing with different colorful flowers blooming all around. The endangered Black Buck deer is found here in plenty. In fact, the park has estimated 400 deer in its expanse. Apart from the Black Bucks, there are many other species of animals here, including Cheetahs, Wild Boar, Monitor Lizards, Mongooses and Porcupines. Regarding avifauna, there are different varieties of Partridges, Quails, Peacocks, Doves, Pond Herons, Egrets, Kites, Vultures, Eagle, Kingfishers and Cormorants.

More than 80 species of migratory birds can be seen here. Another rare variety amongst birds is the Short-toed Eagle. The vegetation of the park is rich with flora like Neem, Butea, Bauhinias Accacias and many thorny shrubs. Mahavir Harina Vanasthali National Park also houses an exhibition hall, where different items of the wild life conversation are displayed. This park is closed on Mondays.

Visiting Hours :

09.00 am to 05.30 pm

Entry Fee : Adult - Rs.5/-

Child - Rs.3/-

Ramoji Film City: Welcome to the world's largest film city. A place where you can treat your entire family to an out of the world experience.

LEGEND

- Airlines
- Airport
- Bank
- Beach
- Bird Sanctuary
- Bus Stand
- Church
- Educational Institution
- Hotel / Restaurant
- Government Office
- Hospital
- Mosque
- Miscellaneous
- Places of Intereast
- Police Station
- Post Office
- Shopping
- Taxi Centre
- Temple

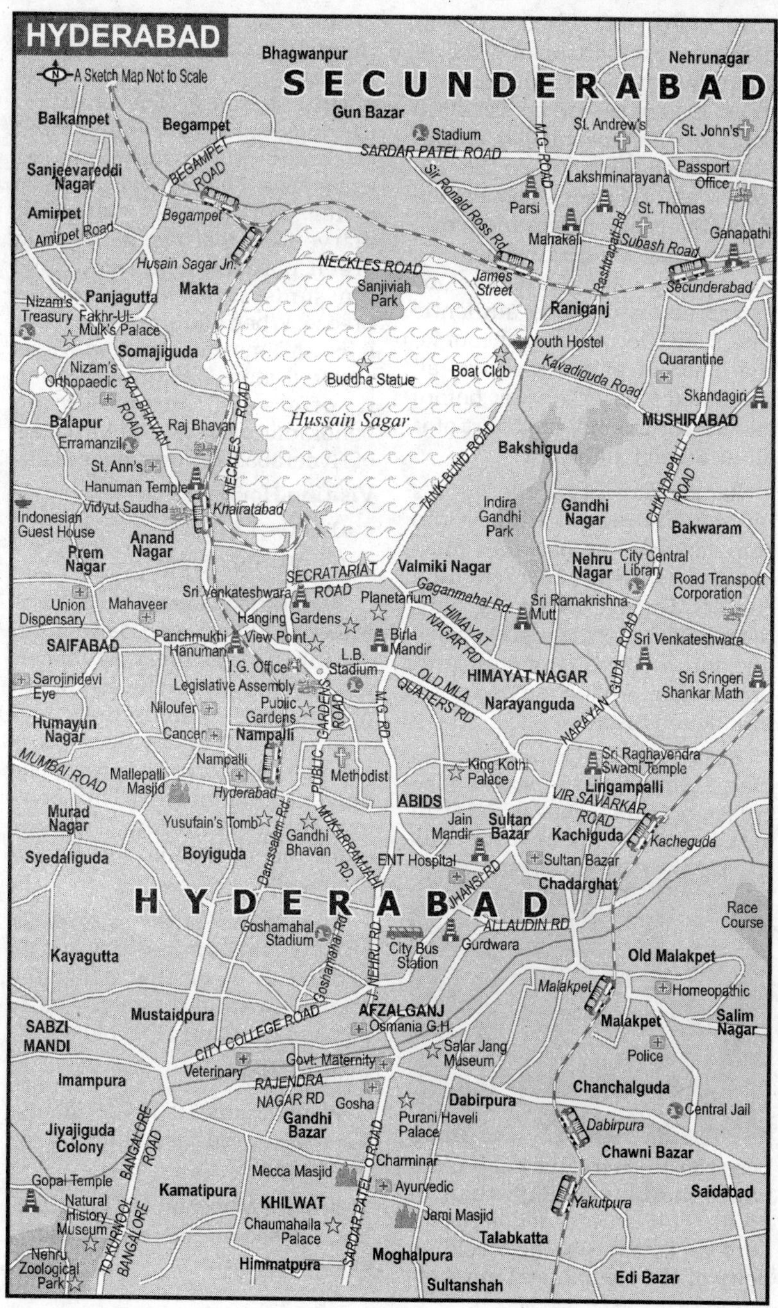
HYDERABAD
A Sketch Map Not to Scale
SECUNDERABAD
Bhagwanpur
Nehrunagar
Gun Bazar
Stadium
SARDAR PATEL ROAD
M.G. ROAD
St. Andrew's
St. John's
Balkampet
Begampet
BEGAMPET ROAD
Sanjeevareddi Nagar
Amirpet
Amirpet Road
Begampet
Sir Ronald Ross Rd.
Parsi
Lakshminarayana
Passport Office
St. Thomas
Mahakali
Rashtrapati Rd.
Subash Road
Ganapathi
Husain Sagar Jn.
NECKLES ROAD
James Street
Secunderabad
Sanjiviah Park
Panjagutta
Makta
Nizam's Treasury
Fakhr-Ul-Mulk's Palace
Raniganj
Youth Hostel
Somajiguda
Kavadiguda Road
Quarantine
Nizam's Orthopaedic
Buddha Statue
Boat Club
Skandagiri
RAJ BHAVAN ROAD
NECKLES ROAD
Hussain Sagar
MUSHIRABAD
Balapur
Raj Bhavan
Erramanzil
TANK BUND ROAD
Bakshiguda
St. Ann's
Hanuman Temple
CHIKADAPALLI ROAD
Vidyut Saudha
Khairatabad
Indira Gandhi Park
Gandhi Nagar
Indonesian Guest House
Bakwaram
Anand Nagar
Prem Nagar
Nehru Nagar
City Central Library
Valmiki Nagar
Road Transport Corporation
SECRATARIAT ROAD
Sri Venkateshwara
Gaganmahal Rd.
Sri Ramakrishna Mutt
Union Dispensary
Mahaveer
Planetarium
HIMAYAT NAGAR RD
Hanging Gardens
Birla Mandir
SAIFABAD
Panchmukhi Hanuman
View Point
NARAYAN GUDA ROAD
Sri Venkateshwara
L.B. Stadium
I.G. Office
Sarojinidevi Eye
Legislative Assembly
OLD MLA QUATERS RD
HIMAYAT NAGAR
Sri Sringeri Shankar Math
Niloufer
Public Gardens
PUBLIC GARDENS ROAD
M.G. RD
Narayanguda
Humayun Nagar
Cancer
Nampalli
Nampalli
Methodist
King Koti Palace
Sri Raghavendra Swami Temple
MUMBAI ROAD
Mallepalli Masjid
Hyderabad
ABIDS
Lingampalli
VIR SAVARKAR ROAD
Murad Nagar
Yusufain's Tomb
Darussalam Rd.
Gandhi Bhavan
MUKARRAMJAHI RD
Jain Mandir
Sultan Bazar
Kachiguda
Kacheguda
Syedaliguda
Boyiguda
ENT Hospital
Sultan Bazar
JHANSI RD
Chadarghat
HYDERABAD
ALLAUDIN RD
Race Course
Goshamahal Stadium
Goshamahal Rd
NEHRU RD
City Bus Station
Gurdwara
Kayagutta
Old Malakpet
Malakpet
Homeopathic
Mustaidpura
AFZALGANJ
Malakpet
Salim Nagar
SABZI MANDI
CITY COLLEGE ROAD
Osmania G.H.
Salar Jang Museum
Police
Veterinary
Govt. Maternity
Imampura
RAJENDRA NAGAR RD
Chanchalguda
Gosha
Dabirpura
Central Jail
Jiyajiguda Colony
BANGALORE ROAD
Gandhi Bazar
Purani Haveli Palace
Dabirpura
SARDAR PATEL ROAD
Charminar
Chawni Bazar
Gopal Temple
Mecca Masjid
Kamatipura
Ayurvedic
Saidabad
Natural History Museum
KHILWAT
Jami Masjid
Yakutpura
TO KURNOOL BANGALORE
Chaumahalla Palace
Talabkatta
Nehru Zoological Park
Himmatpura
Moghalpura
Sultanshah
Edi Bazar

A different destination– glamour, excitement and more! Everything you'd dream a holiday to be, is here spread across 2000 acres of this spectacular world. Easily accessible, about 25 km from the city of Hyderabad, Ramoji Film City is an enchanting blend of man made wonders and nature's pristine beauty. Scores of extraordinary gardens, authentic sets, lavish locales and of course, the glamour of the settings, all combined to offer a never before experience. Come, be a part of it all at Ramoji Film City.

Ramoji Film City, is the world's largest integrated film studio complex and one of Asia's most popular tourism and recreation centres. For the discerning film-maker, RFC offers comprehensive and international-standard pre-production, production and post-production resources.

Birla Mandir: Overseeing the placid waters of the scenic lake Hussain Sagar, this wonderful structure of worship has

been constructed of the impeccable white marbles of Rajasthan in 1976. This shrine dedicated to Lord Venkateswara, the presiding deity of the temple at Tirumala-Tirupati has in its construction an inspiring combination of the traditional architecture of the north and south. The beautiful carvings, splendid sculpture and the ornate workmanship are par excellence. There are also idols of other deities, all made of marvellous marble in the lush green gardens with capricious blossoms caressed by gentle breeze. When illuminated at night it is an amazing sight. As it is situated atop a picturesque hill, it offers an overwhelming panoramic view of the twin cities of Hyderabad and Secunderabad.

Visiting Hours:

07:00 - 12:00 Noon

02:00 - 09:00 pm.

B.M. Birla Planetarium/Science Museum: This exciting Planetarium equipped with most advanced technologies takes the visitors to new heights of amusement and amazement. It offers the viewers a considerable part of the mysterious universe in a 'nutshell'. It opens up vistas in Astronomy. The show glues the spellbound viewers to their seats.

The 'Science Museum' displays various fathomless facets of science. It inculcates a flair for science in young minds. And it inspires the young and old alike.

Visiting Hours:

Planetarium: 10:30 - 15:00 hrs. (Closed on the last Thursday of every month)

Science Museum: 10:30 - 20:15 hrs. (Closed on the last Thursday of every month)

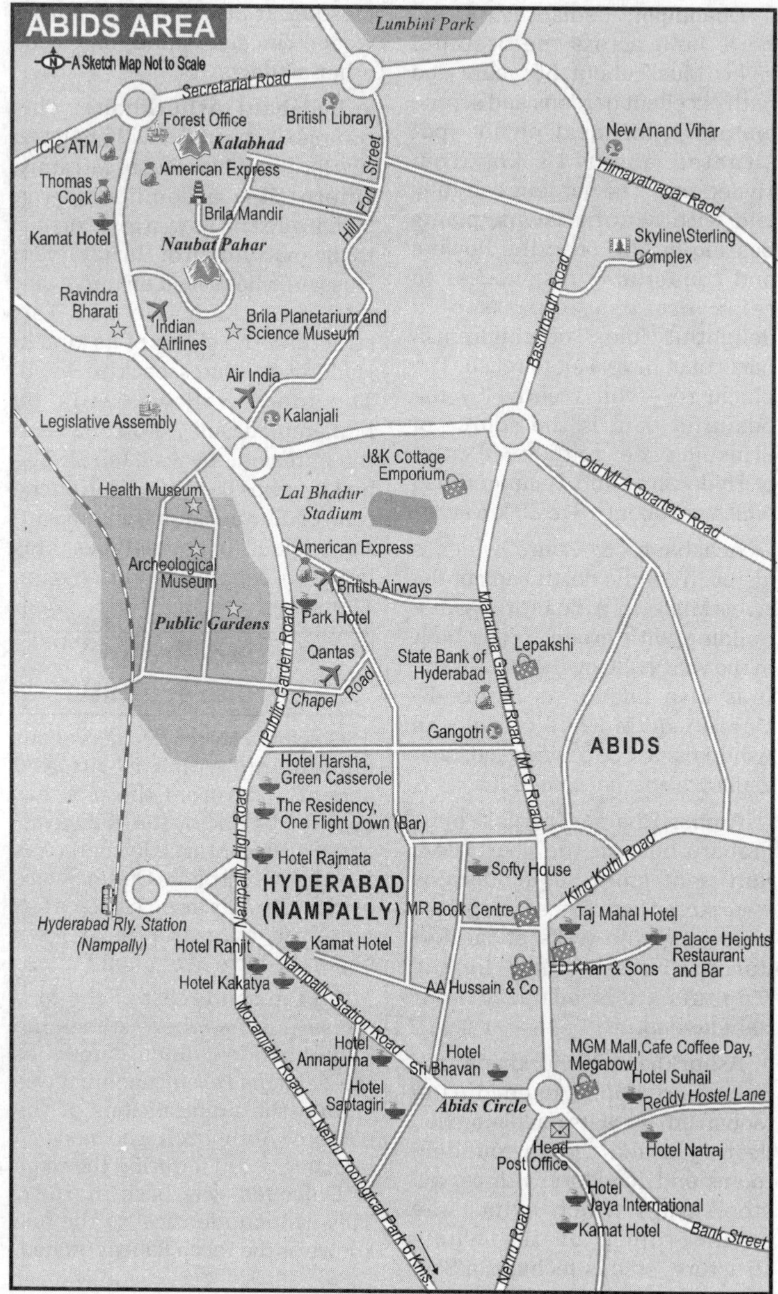

ABIDS AREA
A Sketch Map Not to Scale
Lumbini Park
Secretariat Road
Forest Office
British Library
ICIC ATM
Kalabhad
American Express
Thomas Cook
Brila Mandir
Hill Fort Street
Kamat Hotel
Naubat Pahar
New Anand Vihar
Himayatnagar Raod
Skyline\Sterling Complex
Ravindra Bharati
Indian Airlines
Brila Planetarium and Science Museum
Bashirbagh Road
Air India
Kalanjali
Legislative Assembly
J&K Cottage Emporium
Old MLA Quarters Road
Health Museum
Lal Bhadur Stadium
American Express
Archeological Museum
British Airways
Park Hotel
Public Gardens
(Public Garden Road)
Mahatma Gandhi Road (M G Road)
Qantas
State Bank of Hyderabad
Lepakshi
Chapel Road
Gangotri
ABIDS
Hotel Harsha, Green Casserole
The Residency, One Flight Down (Bar)
Nampally High Road
Hotel Rajmata
Softy House
King Kothi Road
HYDERABAD (NAMPALLY)
MR Book Centre
Taj Mahal Hotel
Hyderabad Rly. Station (Nampally)
Hotel Ranjit
Kamat Hotel
Palace Heights Restaurant and Bar
FD Khan & Sons
Hotel Kakatya
AA Hussain & Co
Nampally Station Road
Mozamjahi Road
Hotel Annapurna
Hotel Sri Bhavan
MGM Mall, Cafe Coffee Day, Megabowl
Hotel Suhail
Reddy Hostel Lane
Hotel Saptagiri
Abids Circle
Head Post Office
Hotel Natraj
To Nehru Zoological Park 6 Kms.
Hotel Jaya International
Kamat Hotel
Bank Street
Nehru Road

Ghandipet: '*Osmansagar Dam*', here, built across the beautiful river 'Musi' about 55 years ago with excellent gardens and serene waters is an ideal picnic spot situated about 18 km from Hyderabad. The gardens carefully laid with alluring lawns, plants bearing bright, beautiful flowers and comfortable rest houses to relax promise tourists of a delightful time. The children in particular, have a lot to relish. The placid reservoir created by the beautiful dam is the source of drinking water to the twin cities of Hyderabad and Secunderabad which are about 18 to 20 km away.

Azakhana - E - Zohra, which is visible from the north bank of the river Musi, in a beautiful white building with green tombs built in the year 1930 by the last Nizam. It is also known as Madre-E-Deccan or Mother of Deccan Ashurkhana. The ceilings and inner walls are enamel coated.

Amber Khana: This is a huge granary built in the year 1642. Sufficient stocks of foodgrains were stored here to feed the people inside the safe walls of the fort during the siege laid by the Moghuls. It is situated near Ramdas Jail.

Ashurkhana: 'Ashurkhana', the mourning house used during Moharrum, with its middle section destroyed and the surrounding rooms and corridors with carved stone trays which evince the ancient glory of the whole structure, stands facing the Safa Mosque. It also houses beautiful wooden incense stands and some other artifacts.

Badshahi Ashurkhana: This complex comprises wide halls *ad hoc* for the 'Shia' sect of Muslims, where they assemble during Moharrum and mourn in reverence to the martyrdom of Hazrat Imam Hussain who played an important role in the Karbala battle. This structure, the oldest of its kind in Hyderabad, dates back to 1596. The inner wall was built by Muhammad Quli Qutub Shah and the outer hall by Asif Jah II. The building was beautified during the rule of Sultan Muhammad with some beautiful enamel tiles. This building remains open only on Thursdays.

In and Around Secunderabad

Golconda Fort: This marvellous monument, which is situated about 11 km from the city, has been left behind by the 'Kakatiyas' of the 13th century. Golconda was also the capital of the Qutub Shahis of the 16th century. The place has emerged over the years as a popular centre of diamond trade.

On the south-east of the fort, 'Musa Burj' is where stands the huge historic cannon, known as the *Azhdaha Paikar* cannon. It was among the ammunitions of the emperor Aurangzeb who made an effective use of it during the siege of Golconda way back in 1687. This cannon identical to the one known as the Faech Rahbar cannon, on the north-west of Golconda Fort was capable of firing shots of 40 kgs in weight.

Qutub Shahi Tombs: About a kilometer from the fort, these beautiful tombs of Qutub Shahi rulers reflect the third and final stage of the 17th century architecture. These tombs are

dome topped and have a square base surrounded by pointed arches. There are galleries of one storey and two stories in these tombs. The domes were originally over-laid with blue and green tiles of which only a few seem to have survived the test of time.

Visiting Hours: 09:30 - 16:30 hrs. (Closed on Fridays)

Salarjung Museum: This exciting Museum is named after the Prime Minister of the erstwile Nizams, Salarjung III who constructed it. A number of ancient articles of arts and paintings of different parts of the

world can be seen here. An exquisite room displays the paraphernalia of historic emperors like Aurangzeb, Tipu Sultan, Shah Jahan, Asaf Jahis, etc.

Visiting Hours: 10:00 - 17:00 hrs. (Closed on Fridays)

Paigah Tombs: Located at Santhosh Nagar, these tombs are

made out of lime and mortar with beautiful inlaid marble carvings. These tombs are 200 years old.

Asman Garh Palace: This grand palace, named after its builder Sir Asman Jah, a noble from the Paigah family, who was also the Prime Minister of Hyderabad state, is located on a beautiful hillock. Granite structures and arched windows mark the grand structure.

Lumbini Park: This is a relatively new park in a historically old city. It offers excellent amusement crowned by a fascinating fountain show in which waters dance to the music.

Visiting Hours: 9:00 - 21:00 hrs. (Closed on Mondays)

Fountain Show:18:30 - 20:00 hrs.

Falaknuma Palace: Italian architecture is reflected in this beautiful palace built by Sir Vikar Ul Umra. Nizam IV bought this wonderful palace in 1897. The palace covers an area of 9,39,712 sq.mtrs, has won international acclaim for its grandeur. This magnificent palace with its huge hall studded with precious stones, stands on a beautiful hill. Situated about 5 km from Charminar, this palace houses some rare treasures collected by the Nizam but it is not open to visitors.

Purani Haveli: This palace, situated in the old city, was the abode of sixth Nizam, 'Purani Haveli' stands for 'Old Mansion'. This palace is of 18th century European style in architecture. Certain old Western style furniture can be seen here. The marvellous wardrobe made of wood built by Mir Mahboob Ali is probably the longest of its kind in the world. It measures to 240 ft in length. Nawab Mukkaram Jah Bahadur donated this palace to Mukkaram Jah Trust in 1971 for educational purposes.

Raymond's Tomb: This tomb of Michael Raymond, a French mercenary who served as a commander in the military of the second Nizam, is situated at Saroornagar in East Hyderabad. It is closed on Fridays

Visiting Hrs :09.30 am - 04.30 pm

Nehru Zoological Park: Named after the first Prime Minister of

India, Pandit Sri Jawaharlal Nehru, this fascinating area spreads over 300 acres and is rated among the largest ones in Asia. A wide variety of captivating bird and animal species, over 300 at a rough estimate, roam about in the park. The lion safari which offers the opportunity to the eager tourists to come face to face with the majestic kings of the jungle, is a special attraction.

The 'nocturnal zoo' an exclusive entity which minds the upkeep of those creatures which are naturally adapted to remain active at nights and retire during the daytime, is one of the salient features here. A special lighting system which simulates a bright moon enables the visitors to catch a glimpse of the exciting nocturnal

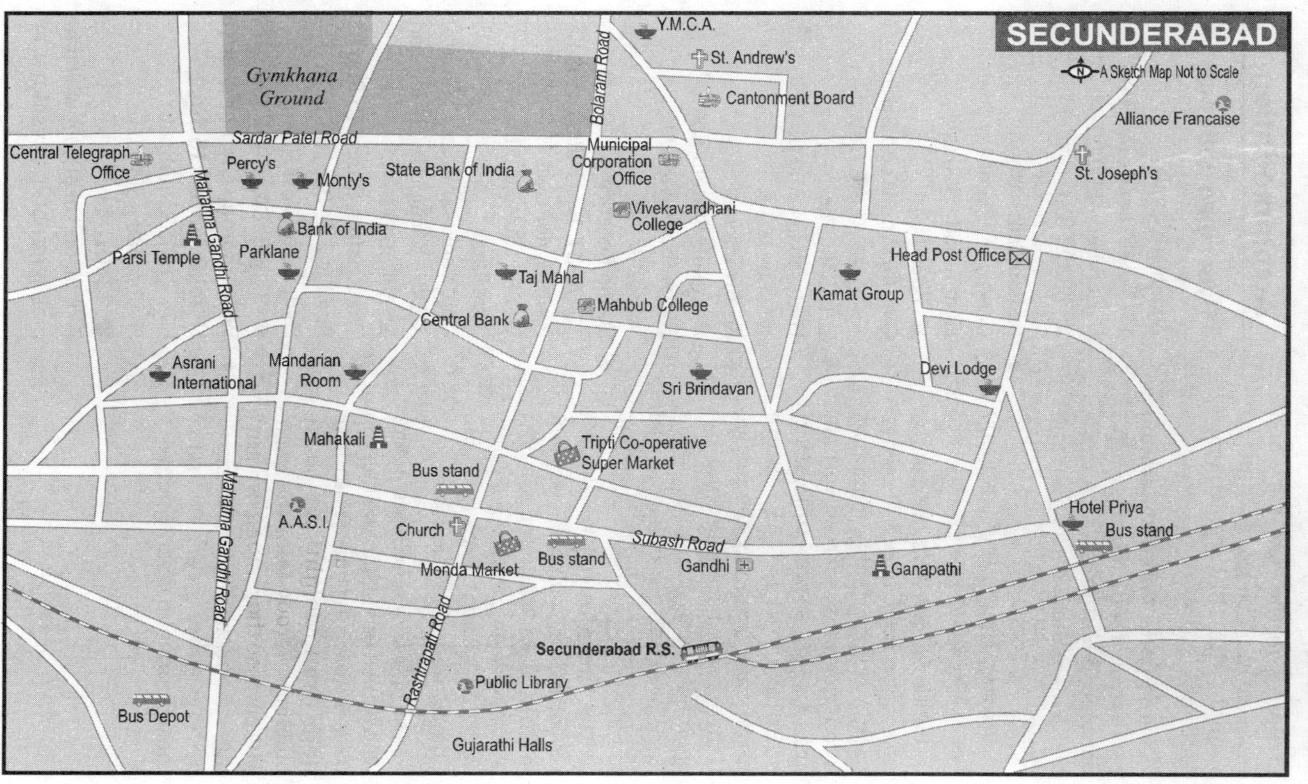
SECUNDERABAD
A Sketch Map Not to Scale
Y.M.C.A.
St. Andrew's
Cantonment Board
Alliance Francaise
St. Joseph's
Gymkhana Ground
Bolaram Road
Sardar Patel Road
Central Telegraph Office
Percy's
Monty's
State Bank of India
Municipal Corporation Office
Vivekavardhani College
Bank of India
Parsi Temple
Parklane
Mahatma Gandhi Road
Taj Mahal
Head Post Office
Kamat Group
Mahbub College
Central Bank
Asrani International
Mandarian Room
Sri Brindavan
Devi Lodge
Mahakali
Tripti Co-operative Super Market
Bus stand
A.A.S.I.
Church
Hotel Priya
Bus stand
Subash Road
Bus stand
Monda Market
Gandhi
Ganapathi
Mahatma Gandhi Road
Rashtrapati Road
Secunderabad R.S.
Public Library
Bus Depot
Gujarathi Halls

creatures in the day. Rare and interesting creatures can be seen in the 'Natural History Museum'.

Large parks with exhilarating recreation facilities, beautiful gardens, pleasure rides on mini-train all enhance the fun and cheer.

Visiting Hours: 09:00 - 17:00 hrs. (Closed on Mondays)

Public Gardens: Situated in the city-centre and formerly known as Bagh-e-aam, the public gardens is a conscientiously carved verdant area with some important buildings like the State Legislature, Assembly, the Jubilee Hall, the Jawahar Bal Bhavan, the open-air theatre known as 'Lalita Kala Toranam', the archaeological Museum and the Health Museum.

The 'State Museum' here houses rare artefacts, sculptures, ancient inscriptions, old age coins, a host of armoury and traditional crafts such as Bidri articles, old Chinaware and textiles.

The offices of two Hindu nobles who served under Tanah Shah can be seen above the guard lines. Two huge iron weights in these buildings sprout from the sand. The purpose they served, whether they were intended to remain exactly in the way they are and things like that continue to be an enigma.

Accommodation

Hyderabad (STD : 040)

- **Ayodhya**
  11-5-427, Lakdi-Ka-Pool,
  Hyderabad - 500 004
  ☎: 23393420
- **Badam Balakrishna**
  6-1-1081, Lakdi-Ka-Pool,
  Hyderabad - 500 004
  ☎: 23231652
- **Comfort Inn Wood Bridge**
  11-4-649/C, AC Guards,
  Lakdi-Ka-Pool,
  Hyderabad - 500 004.
  ☎: 66610015
- **Sri Brindavan**
  Nampalli Station Road,
  Hyderabad - 500 001.
  ☎: 23203970
- **Sudha Regency**
  11-5-431, Red Hills, Lakdi-Ka-Pool, Hyderabad - 500 004.
  ☎: 23315696 (10 lines)
- **Suprabhat**
  Opp. Venkataramana Theatre,
  3-3-50, Kachiguda, Hyderabad.
  ☎: 66615111
- **The Krishna Oberoi (5 Star)**
  Road No. 1, Banjara Hills,
  Hyderabad - 300 034.
  ☎: 23392323, Fax: 23393079
- **Welcomgroup Grand Kakatiya Hotel & Towers (5 Star)**
  6-3-1187, Begumpet,
  Hyderabad - 500 016.
  ☎: 23401045
  E-mail: gn.kakatiya@welcome mail.wiprobt.ems.vsnl.net.in

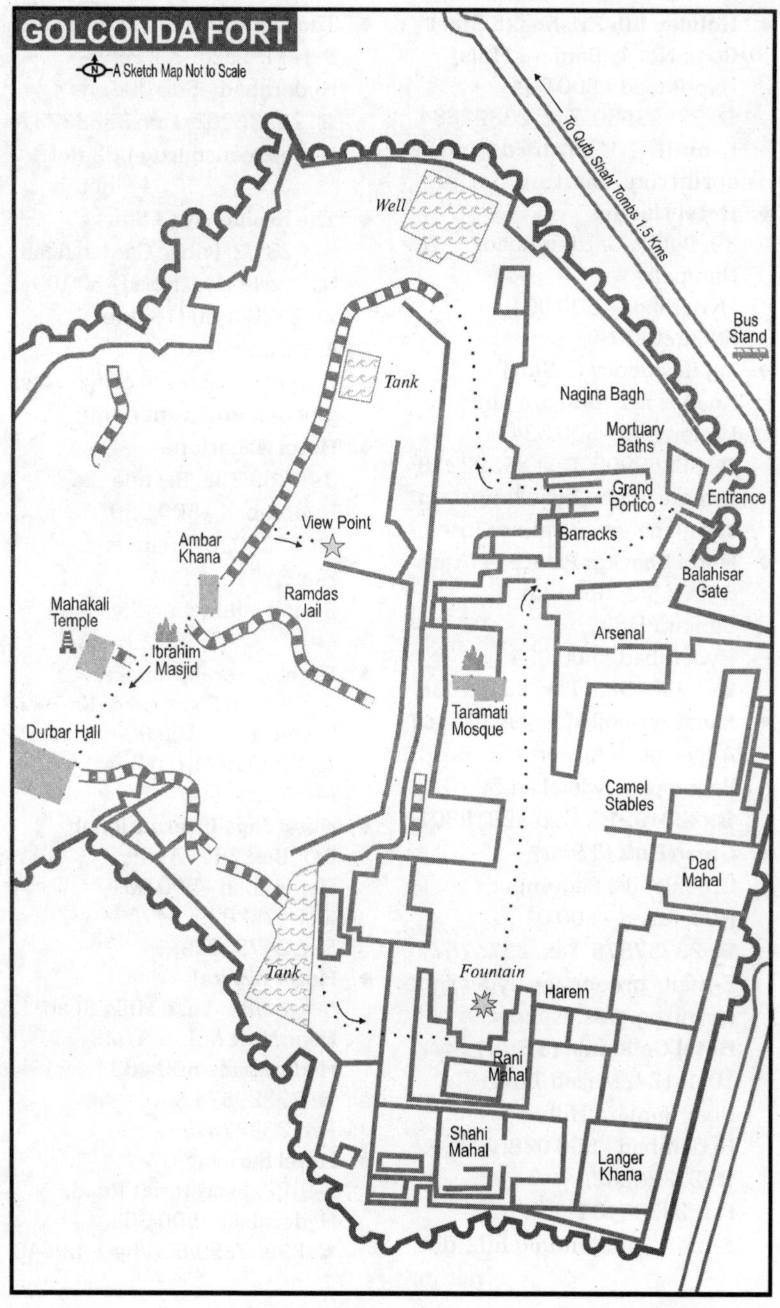
GOLCONDA FORT
A Sketch Map Not to Scale
Well
To Qutb Shahi Tombs 1.5 Kms
Bus Stand
Tank
Nagina Bagh
Mortuary Baths
Grand Portico
Entrance
View Point
Barracks
Ambar Khana
Balahisar Gate
Ramdas Jail
Mahakali Temple
Ibrahim Masjid
Arsenal
Taramati Mosque
Durbar Hall
Camel Stables
Dad Mahal
Tank
Fountain
Harem
Rani Mahal
Shahi Mahal
Langer Khana

- **Holiday Inn Krishna (5 Star)**
Road No. 1, Banjara Hills,
Hyderabad - 500 034.
☎: 23393939, Fax: 23392684
E-mail: hilk@hyd@rml.
sprintrpg.ems.vsnl.net.in
- **Hotel Harsha**
39, Public Garden Road,
Nampally,
Hyderabad - 500 001.
☎: 23202714
- **Taj Residency (5 Star)**
Road No. 1, Banjara Hills,
Hyderabad - 500 034.
☎: 66669999, Fax: 23392218
E-mail: trhbc.hya@tajgroup.
sprintrpg.ems.vsnl.net.in
- **Hotel Bhaskar Palace (4 Star)**
6-3-248/2, Road No. 1,
Banjara Hills,
Hyderabad - 500 034.
☎: 23301523, Fax: 23304036
- **Ramada Hotel Manohar (4 Star)**
Adjacent to Airport Exit Road,
Begumpet,Hyderabad-500 016.
☎: 22819917, Fax: 22819801
- **Green Park (3 Star)**
Greenlands, Begumpet,
Hyderabad - 500 016.
☎: 23757575 Fax: 23757677
E-mail: greenpark.hyd@rml.
sprintrpg.ems.vsnl.net.in
- **Hotel Golkonda (3 Star)**
10-1-124, Masab Tank,
Near Banjara Hills,
Hyderabad - 500 028.
☎: 23320202,
Fax: 23320404
E-mail: golkonda@hd2.dot.
net.in
- **The Central Court Hotel (3 Star)**
6-1-71, Lakdi-Ka-Pool,
Hyderabad - 500 004.
☎: 23233262, Fax: 23232737
E-mail: cencourt@hd2.dot.
net.in
- **The Residency (3 Star)**
5-8-231/2, Public Garden Road,
Nampally, Hyderabad - 500 001.
☎: 23204060 (18 lines)
Fax: 23204040
E-mail: tres.hot@gmyd.tres.
globalet.ems.vsnl.net.in
- **Hotel Nagarjuna**
3-6-356/358, Basheer Bagh,
Hyderabad - 500 029.
☎: 23220201 (9 lines)
Fax: 27714911
E-mail: afl.hyd.neehyd.xee
mail
- **Hotel Dwaraka Palace**
Raj Bhavan Road, Lakdi-Ka-Pool,
Hyderabad - 500 004.
☎: 22237921 (10 lines)
Fax: 22211900
- **Hotel Jaya International**
P.O. Box 264, Abids,
Hyderabad - 500 001.
☎: 24752929, 24757483
Fax: 24753919
- **Hotel Krystal**
5-9-24/82, Lake Hills Road,
Near New M.L.A. QMS,
Hyderabad - 500 463.
☎: 23229874
Fax: 23227877
- **Hotel Sarovar**
5-9-22, Secretariat Road,
Hyderabad - 500 063.
☎: 22237299/638/640-42/648

- **Hotel Rajmata**
  5-8-230, Nampally,
  Hyderabad - 500 001.
  ☎: 23201000/21, 23203222
  Fax: 23204133
- **Blue Moon Hotel**
  6-3-1186/A, Rajbhavan Road,
  Begumpet, Hyderabad - 500 016.
  ☎: 23312815 Fax: 23321700
- **Hotel Rajdhani**
  15-1-503, Siddiamber Bazaar,
  Hyderabad - 500 012.
  ☎: 24740651 (11 lines)
- **Hotel Sangeetha International**
  Panjagutta "x" Roads,
  Above Shanbagh Hotel,
  Hyderabad - 500 482.
  ☎: 23312142, 26502142
- **Hotel Dwaraka Deluxe**
  Lakdi-Ka-Pool,
  Hyderabad - 500 004.
  ☎: 23297392, 22242444
  E-mail:dwaraka@hotmail.com
- **Neo Hotel Haridwar**
  4-6-465, Esamiya Bazaar,
  Hyderabad - 500 027.
  ☎: 24656711/18 Fax: 24732780
- **Shree Venkateswara Lodge**
  6-1-74, Lakdi-Ka-Pool,
  Hyderabad - 500 004.
  ☎: 22236871 (6 lines)
  Fax: 22235914
- **The Royal Hotel**
  5-8-225, Opp. Nampally Railway Station,
  Hyderabad-1.
  ☎: 23202998, 23204111
- **Viceroy**
  Opp. Hussain Sagar Lake,
  Tankbund Road,
  Hyderabad-80.
  ☎: 27538383 Fax: 27538797
  E-mail: viceroy@hdl.vsnl.net.in
- **Hotel Gopi**
  5-8-108,Opp Nampally Station,
  Hyderabad - 500001.
  ☎: 23205550
- **Shahran Hotel**
  22-6-131 Machili Kaman,
  Near Charminar,
  Hyderabad - 500002.
  ☎: 24576080
- **Rock Castle Hotel**
  8-2-410 Road No.6, Banjara Hills,
  Hyderabad - 500034.
  ☎: 23352843
- **Mujeeb Hotel**
  7-1-307/15 Subhash Nagar,
  Sanatnagar, Opp. To Swamy Theatre, Hyderabad - 500018.
  ☎: 23704135
- **Village Inns (India) Ltd**
  8-2-472/1, Road No. 5, Banjara Hills, Near Sapal Cement,
  Hyderabad - 500034.
  ☎: 23356683
- **Kartikeya Inn (Boorgu Group)**
  15-2-719 To 724 N S Road,
  Osmangunj, Hyderabad - 500012.
  ☎: 55634445
- **Madhura Biryani House**
  8-3-214/A/Lv Srinivas Nagar,
  West Hyderabad - 500000.
  ☎: 23737194
- **Kamat Lingapur Hotel**
  1-10-44/2 Chikoti Gardens,
  Begumpet, Hyderabad - 500016.
  ☎: 27764059
- **Macca Hotel**
  Mozam Jahi Market,
  Opp Cdr Hospital,
  Hyderabad - 500001.
  ☎: 24606283

- **Jai Hind Hotel (Pt)**
  23-5-1176 G Pura Pathergatti,
  Next To Sudha Theatre,
  Hyderabad - 500002.
  ☎: 24531053
- **Hotel Watan Residency**
  15-1-522-25, Watan Plaza,
  Siddiamber Bazar,
  Hyderabad - 500012.
  ☎: 24658438
- **Hotel Vishnu Priya**
  6-3-658/16/A,
  Erra Manzil Main Road,
  Somajiguda,
  Opp Civil Supplies B,
  Hyderabad - 500082.
  ☎: 66255657
- **Hotel Vishnu**
  6-14-1081/82 Lakdikapool,
  Hyderabad - 500004.
  ☎: 22233823
- **Hotel Vaibhav**
  5-4-11 Nr Gpo Abid,
  Near Petrol Pump,
  Hyderabad - 500001.
  ☎: 24606610
- **Hotel Urvasi**
  6-3-665/A1 Punjagutta,
  Hyderabad - 500082.
  ☎: 23420552, 23420550
- **Hotel Transit**
  1-11-251/21 Airport Road,
  Begumpet,
  Hyderabad - 500016.
  ☎: 27760580
- **Hotel Tapasvi**
  Ist Floor Sobhana Complex,
  Balanagar,
  Hyderabad - 500037.
  ☎: 23771887
- **Hotel Swaraj**
  1-8-524/2 Chikkadpally,
  Hyderabad - 500020.
  ☎: 27661962
- **Hotel Surya Boarding And Lodging**
  9-32 Lalitha Nagar,
  Dilshuk Nagar,
  Opp Shivani Lodge,
  Hyderabad - 500060.
  ☎: 24064104
- **Hotel Sunanda**
  1-8-23/1 Chikkadpally,
  Hyderabad - 500020.
  ☎: 27664479
- **Hotel Suhail**
  4-1-527 Troop Bazar Abids,
  Back Side Ramkrishna Theatre,
  Hyderabad - 500001.
  ☎: 24610299
- **Hotel Sudarshan International**
  Narayanguda,
  Hyderabad - 500029.
  ☎: 23226562
- **Hotel Sri Krishna**
  6-1-1081 Lakdi Ka Pul,
  Hyderabad - 500029.
  ☎: 23230156

Accommodation

Secunderabad (STD : 040)

- **Hotel Heritage**
  116, Chenoy Trade Centre,
  Park Lane,
  Secunderabad - 500 003.
  ☎: 27845020,
  Fax: 27841455
  E-mail: tauras@hd1.vsnl.net.in

- **Asrani International Hotel (3 Star)**
  1-7-179, M. G. Road,
  Secunderabad - 500 003.
  ☎: 27842267 (7 lines), 27846401
  Fax: 2846903
- **Hotel Baseraa (3 Star)**
  9-1-167/168, S.D. Road,
  Secunderabad - 500 003.
  ☎: 27703200, Fax: 27704745
- **Hotel Deccan Continental (3 Star)**
  Sir Ronald Ross Road,
  Secunderabad - 500 003.
  ☎: 27840981 (9 lines), 26260990 (3 lines)
  Fax: 27840980
- **Hotel Parklane (P) Ltd**
  115, Park Lane,
  Secunderabad - 500 003.
  ☎: 27840448, 27840399
- **Hotel Ambassador**
  1-7-27, S.D. Road,
  Secunderabad - 500 003.
  ☎: 27843760, 27844774/882
  Fax: 27869095
- **Hotel Karan**
  1-2-261/1, S.D. Road,
  Secunderabad - 500 003.
  ☎: 27840191 (10 lines)
  Fax: 27848343
- **Moti Mahal Hotel**
  8-2-241 St. Marys Road,
  Secunderabad - 500003.
  ☎: 66313103
- **Montgomerys Hotel**
  108 S D Road,
  Secunderabad - 500003.
  ☎: 27844998
- **Metro Hotel**
  48 M G Road Leftside,
  Near Ramgolapet Police Station,
  Secunderabad - 500003.
  ☎: 27843291
- **Masooda Hotel**
  54 Kamasari Bazaar,
  Bowenpally,
  Opp Post Office,
  Secunderabad - 500011.
  ☎: 27751941
- **Kamat Hotel**
  1-7-241 Ramalaya Complex,
  S D Road,
  Near Paradise Circle,
  Secunderabad - 500003.
  ☎: 27840479
- **Hotel Sri Vinayak**
  9-4-130-131 Regimental Bazaar,
  Opp Secunderabad Rly Station,
  Secunderabad - 500025.
  ☎: 27802146

Rangareddy

This district is named after the famous freedom fighter and Telanga leader Sri. Ranga Reddy. This district was earlier included in the Hyderabad district and bifurcated in the year 1978. Rangareddy district has an area of 7,493 Sq.km. and a population of 3,575,064 as of 2001. The forest area is only 9.6% of the district area. Social forestry is making all its efforts in growing Eucalyptus trees and other plants. Quartz is found in many parts of the district. Also, Jambala Clays are available aplenty, which are used in the manufacture of Bricks and Drainage Pipes.This district has an international reputation for its Grapes. Acharya N.G.Ranga Agricultural University (Angrau) at Rajendranagar has won many credits and recognized as the best university at the National Level.

Medium Scale Industries and Cement Corporation of India's Cement Factories are established at Tandur. Hyderabad Chemicals and Fertilizers at Moula-Ali established in 1942 are to name few. Osman Sagar, a Fresh Water reservoir is the Prime Drinking Water source to the Capital City of Hyderabad. Agriculture University is established at Rajendernagar in this district where research operations for getting more yields are taking place.

Anantagiri Hill Station: Anantagiri is a famous hill station in Ranga Reddy, located 70 km from Hyderabad. Andhra Pradesh Tourism Development Corporation Ltd has prepared a master plan to develop this hill station. The proposed 200-acre hill resort will have a business park with conferencing facility besides a healthcare centre, adventure club and recreational units like open theatre and multi-cuisine restaurants. The corporation also plans to develop a common entrance plaza, public utilities and other basic infrastructure facilities.

Himayat Sagar: This lake is 20 kilometers distant from the Hyderabad city. This is a picturesque lake that supplies drinking water to the city. Besides Osmansagar, this reservoir is created to overcome the flooding of the Musi. Both the Himayatsagar on the Musi and Osmanasagar on the Isa were built by Osman Ali Khan, the VII Nizam. The road on the bund of Himayat Sagar lake provides an exhilarating driving experience. The heavenly combination of crisp clean air, sparkling water and lush vegetation will remain evergreen in the memories of tourists.

Osman Sagar: This reservoir created on the River Isa is a tributary of the Musi River that runs through the city. It is a serene picnic spot with lush gardens overlooking the lake. Osmansagar Lake spans over an area of 46 sq km. Nearby is the famous Sagar Mahal guest house, the summer resort of the Nizams, the erstwhile rulers of the region.

Jawahar Lake: This lake in Shamirpet near Hyderabad is an artificial water body that was dug out some 50 years ago or so. The Shamirpet Lake is officially called the Jawahar Lake and is mainly dependent on the rainfalls. This lake also has a dam like contraption near which is located the temple of Katta Maisamma, who also happens to be the patron deity of Shamirpet near Hyderabad. Next to this temple are a pond and a garden. The pond serves as a resting ground for migratory birds. An enchanting picnic spot, it has an adjoining deer park run by the Forest Department.

Chittoor

This district abounds in ancient temples with astounding architecture and hence has a number of pilgrim centres. The famous 'Sri Venkateswara Temple' here, attracts millions of devotees all through the year from far and wide. This temple receives the maximum pecuniary offerings, of all the worship centres in the world. The origin of this ancient temple is still a moot point among archaeologists and the religious heads. The Lord here has been worshipped by a number of rulers, saints and monks in the long past. The vast environs of the temple and the 'Seven Hills' of sublime beauty are considered sacred. There are also countless number of ancient temples in and around Tirupati. At 'Alamelumangapuram', a marvellous temple is dedicated to Goddess Padmavathi, the consort of 'Lord Venkateswara'. The Siva temple at Sri Kalahasthi, also an ancient one, is one of the five exclusive group of Temples known as the 'Panchaboothakshethra'. Nagalapuram and Narayanavanam have ancient temples too and interesting legends. The antique temples at Ramagiri, set in a scenic sylvan location recount interesting legends. The temple tank here is watered by a perennial spring which caters to drinking water and agrarian needs.

The Vijayanagara influence is largely felt in the district. The massive fort at Chandragiri believed to have been built in 1000

AD has been renovated by the later Vijanagara rulers.

There are also exciting picnic spots. The KalyaniDam, one such spot, located about 18 km from Tirupati regulates the drinking water supply to the town of Tirupati. Horsley Hills is a cool resort in the hot seasons. Graced by benevolent ambience and picturesque scenery of this hill forms part of the mighty 'Eastern Ghats'. This place has been in the focus of tourism ever since it was discovered in 1870 and named after its discoverer W.D. Horsley. The Gurrumkonda Hills is also an enchanting hill resort.

Temples In and Around Tirupati

Sri Venkateswara Swamy Temple: This famous ancient temple dedicated to 'Lord Venkateswara' also faithfully adored by other names as 'Venkatesa', 'Balaji', 'Venkata-ramana', 'Govinda', 'Srinivasa' and so on is ideally situated on the top of a cluster of seven sacred hills reverentially personified as the seven mammoth hoods of the mythical serpent 'Adisesha' whose numerous coils represent the limitless 'Time' as a cosmic concept. 'Lord Venkateswara,' the presiding deity here is one of the various forms of 'Lord Vishnu', the protector of the Universe, who reposes on the body of 'Adisesha'.

The exact date of the construction of the ancient temple is yet to be discerned. However, history cites the town of Tirupati to have come into existence in the 12th century. The temple with excellent

architecture has been worshipped by several heroes of the Pallava, Chola, Pandya and Vijayanagara dynasties and later by the rulers of Mysore. The Vimanam or the dome over the Sanctum Sanctorum and the Dwajasthambam are completely gold plated. The temple at an altitude of about 853 m above sea level with its picturesque environs and tranquil ambience is indisputably a Heaven on Earth. The temple can be reached both by vehicle and on foot from Tirupati. The foot path is 15 km long with a flight of rock cut steps.

This Holy place has repeatedly been visited by a number of saints, monks, religious reformers and the like in the long history.

There are references to this temple in the ancient literary works of Tamil.

Anointing the deity with camphor and the devotees having their head tonsured are two impor-

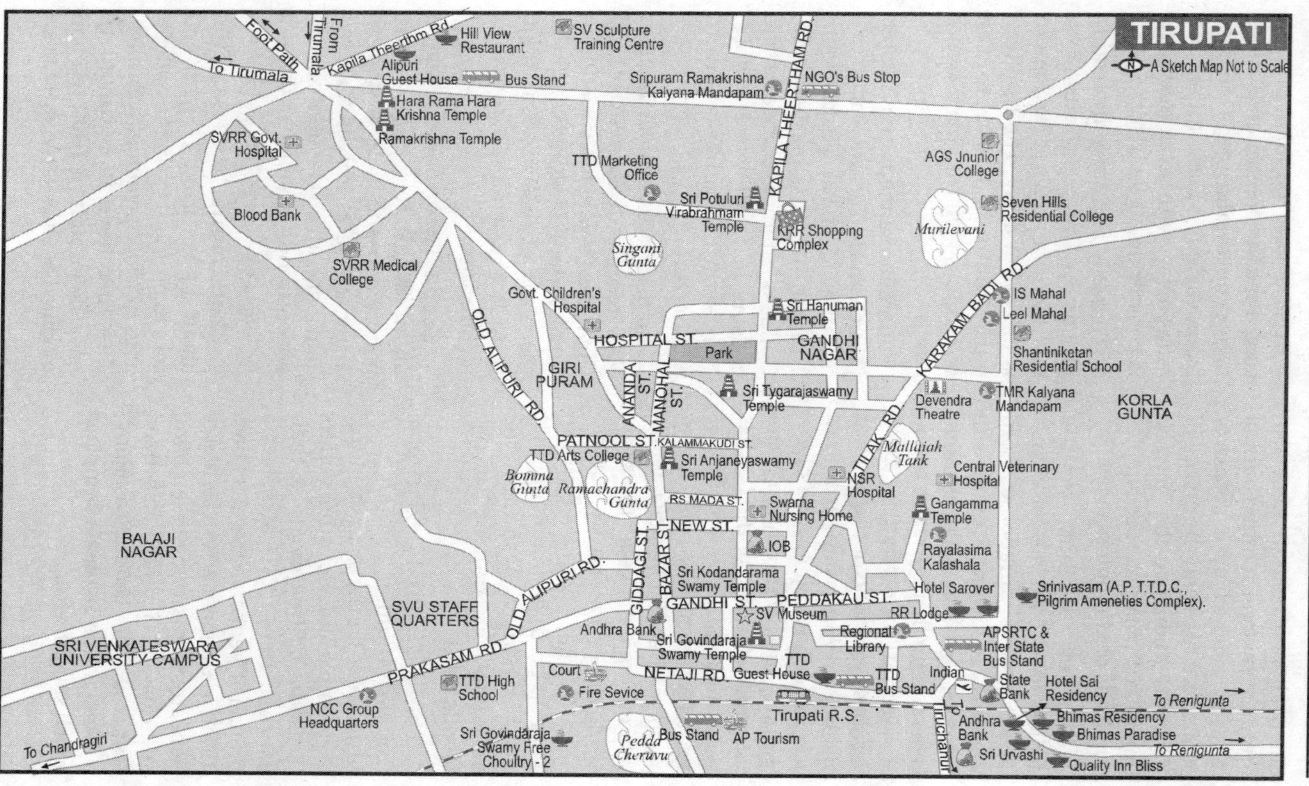
TIRUPATI
A Sketch Map Not to Scale
From Tirumala
Foot Path
To Tirumala
Kapila Theerthm Rd.
Hill View Restaurant
SV Sculpture Training Centre
Alipuri Guest House
Bus Stand
Sripuram Ramakrishna Kalyana Mandapam
NGO's Bus Stop
Hara Rama Hara Krishna Temple
Ramakrishna Temple
SVRR Govt. Hospital
Blood Bank
SVRR Medical College
TTD Marketing Office
Sri Potuluri Virabrahmam Temple
KAPILA THEERTHAM RD.
KRR Shopping Complex
Singani Gunta
AGS Jnunior College
Seven Hills Residential College
Murilevani
KARAKAM BADI RD.
IS Mahal
Leel Mahal
Shantiniketan Residential School
Govt. Children's Hospital
Sri Hanuman Temple
HOSPITAL ST.
Park
GANDHI NAGAR
OLD ALIPURI RD.
GIRI PURAM
ANANDA ST.
MANOHAL ST.
Sri Tygarajaswamy Temple
Devendra Theatre
TMR Kalyana Mandapam
KORLA GUNTA
TILAK RD.
PATNOOL ST.
KALAMMAKUDI ST.
TTD Arts College
Sri Anjaneyaswamy Temple
Mallaiah Tank
NSR Hospital
Central Veterinary Hospital
Bomma Gunta
Ramachandra Gunta
RS MADA ST.
Swarna Nursing Home
Gangamma Temple
NEW ST.
IOB
Rayalasima Kalashala
BALAJI NAGAR
GIDDAGI ST.
BAZAR ST.
ALIPURI RD.
Sri Kodandarama Swamy Temple
Hotel Sarover
Srinivasam (A.P. T.T.D.C., Pilgrim Ameneties Complex).
GANDHI ST.
PEDDAKAU ST.
SV Museum
RR Lodge
SVU STAFF QUARTERS
Andhra Bank
Sri Govindaraja Swamy Temple
Regional Library
APSRTC & Inter State Bus Stand
SRI VENKATESWARA UNIVERSITY CAMPUS
PRAKASAM RD.
Court
TTD Guest House
NETAJI RD.
TTD Bus Stand
Indian
State Bank
Hotel Sai Residency
To Renigunta
TTD High School
Fire Sevice
Tirupati R.S.
NCC Group Headquarters
Tiruchanur
Andhra Bank
Bhimas Residency
Bhimas Paradise
Sri Govindaraja Swamy Free Choultry - 2
Pedda Cheruvu
Bus Stand
AP Tourism
Sri Urvashi
Quality Inn Bliss
To Chandragiri

tant traditional customs here. The Brahmotsavam is a grand annual festival marked by a series of poojas and rites and the arrival of 'Tirupati Kodai' or the 'Sacred Umbrella' from numerous temples hundreds of kilometers away.

Another ancient temple dedicated to 'Lord Varahaswamy' who is again a variation of 'Lord Vishnu', is situated along the 'Temple Tank' called 'Pushkarani'. Legend has it that the entire region of Tirupati is owned by Lord Varahaswami who at the request of Lord Venkateswara had accommodated him in the place. Hence, the 'Neivedyam', the customary feeding of the Lord, is performed at this temple first as also a few other rites, before being performed at the Venkateswaraswamy temple. A belief rules that all devotees willing to worship Lord Venkateswara ought to worship Lord Varahaswamy first since it had been so arranged between the deities in the Mythical era.

The 'Tirumala Tirupati Devasthanam' which is responsible for the maintenance of this temple and a lot others offers 'Prasada' or free meals at their canteen here. TTD also has a branch at Venkatanarayana Road, T.Nagar, Chennai where an idol of Venkateswaraswamy resembling the one at Tirumala has been installed. The 'Laddu Prasadam', a sweet at the Tirumala Temple is much sought-after.

It is a very popular pilgrim centre and the number of devotees taking on a pilgrimage on foot from various spots, miles and miles away, with strict austerity, is constantly on the rise.

There are also other interesting places in the proximity. The ravishing waterfalls at Papanasam is just 8 km away. The beautiful park about 4 km from the temple is a favourite hang-out to many.

Alamelumangapuram Temple (Tiruchanur) : This ancient temple is situated about 10 km from Tirupati. The presiding deity here, Goddess Alamelumanga is the consort of Lord Venkateswara. This temple holds a grand architecture.

Govindaraja Perumal Temple: This temple dedicated to Lord Govindaraja who is a variation of 'Lord Vishnu' is situated right in the heart of the city. This huge temple is rich in ancient architecture.

Kapila Theertham: Situated about 2 km from 'Alipiri', the point where the flight of steps to Tirumala starts, this is a sacred Tank beneath an elevated rock on which stands a temple dedicated to Lord Siva.

Chandragiri: It is situated about 11 km from Tirupati and rose to prominence in the twilight days of the Vijayanagara Empire. The fort here is believed to have been built in 1000 AD and modified by the later Vijayanagara

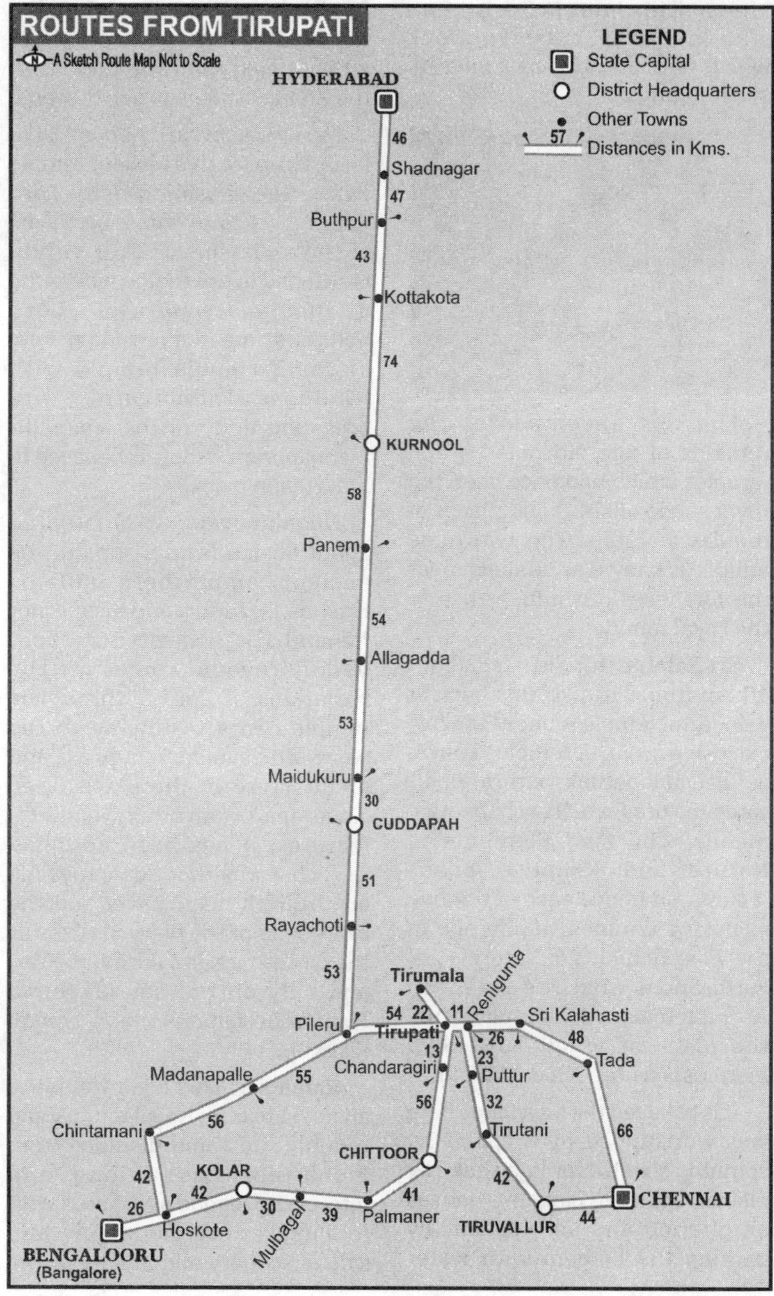
ROUTES FROM TIRUPATI
A Sketch Route Map Not to Scale
LEGEND
State Capital
District Headquarters
Other Towns
57
Distances in Kms.
HYDERABAD
46
Shadnagar
47
Buthpur
43
Kottakota
74
KURNOOL
58
Panem
54
Allagadda
53
Maidukuru
30
CUDDAPAH
51
Rayachoti
53
Tirumala
Renigunta
Pileru
54
22
11
Tirupati
Sri Kalahasti
26
48
Tada
13
23
Chandaragiri
Puttur
Madanapalle
55
56
32
Tirutani
Chintamani
56
66
CHITTOOR
42
KOLAR
42
42
41
CHENNAI
26
30
39
Palmaner
44
Hoskote
TIRUVALLUR
Mulbagal
BENGALOORU
(Bangalore)

kings. This magnificent fort stands on a massive rock which is about 182 m above its surroundings.

The fort encompasses the remains of age-old palaces and temples which had once been the royal abode of kings and places of regular worship. The two huge buildings known as 'Mahals' near the fort were of multiple use to the royal family.

Sri Kalahasthi: Situated about 40 km from Tirupati this ancient wonderful temple is one of the five exclusive group of temples known as 'Panchaboothakshethra' dedicated to Lord Siva. 'Panchabootha' means 'The Five Elements of Nature' and 'Kshetra' means 'Place' and hence each of the five exclusive temples signify one of the 'Five Elements of Nature' (Viz) Earth, Space, Wind, Fire and Water. As this temple is the 'Vayukshetra', the place of wind, Lord Siva manifests as the 'God of Wind'.

It is believed the Siva Linga here was worshipped by a spider by spinning a web over it, a snake by placing upon the Lingam a gem as an offering and an elephant by bathing the Lingam with water from its trunk. And worshipping the Lord here relieves people of difficulties during the periods of the Zodiac Aquarius and Pisces.

Narayanavanam: About 43 km from Tirupati, this ancient temple where the presiding deity Lord Kalyana Venkateswara is again one of the variations of Lord Vishnu is situated in the region where the divine marriage of Lord Venkateswara, the presiding deity of the Tirumala temple with 'Goddess Padmavathi', the presiding deity of the Alamelumangapuram temple is believed to have taken place.

Nagalapuram: It is situated about 65 km from Tirupati. The ancient temple here built by Krishna Devaraya and his mother Nagamba is dedicated to 'Lord Vedanarayana', one of the variations of Lord Vishnu. The temple bears testimony to the wayward development of a grand architecture in the olden days, since, apart from other wonderful features, it has been designed in such a way that Sun's rays fall on the Holy feet, navel and the fore- head of the deity in turns as the day progresses during the day and only on the day of 'Surya Pooja', the famous grand annual festival.

Ramagiri: This beautiful place about 5 km from Nagalapuram and roughly the same distance from Pichattoor has a long and interesting legend associated with it. Picturesque mountains and sylvan scenery add beauty to the place while two ancient temples, one at the foot and the other on the top of a scenic hillock add sanctity to it. This sacred place is also known as '*Bhairava Kshethra*', the 'Abode of Bhairava' as the presiding deity of the hill-foot temple is 'Lord Kalabhairava', one of the various forms of 'Lord Siva' in which the Lord assumes the role of commander of 'Dogs'.

The hill-top temple is dedicated to 'Lord Muruga', the son of the divine couple Lord Siva and Goddess Parvathi and the brother of 'Lord Ganesa', the principal deity in the Elephant-head and Human-body form.

The legend has it that while Lord Anjaneya on an errand bid by Lord Rama was making His way by air to Rameswaram with a Siva Linga taken from Kasi to be installed there carefully placed on His mighty shoulders. He was surprisingly confronted by strange and dry weather with the Sun scorching like never before and the wind blowing against and trying to emulate the air-borne Lord. But this was after all premeditated and perfectly organised by Lord Kalabhairava, the Lord of the land who wanted the Linga to be installed right here at His place. Unaware of this and driven by thirst, Lord Anjaneya went on screening the whole area for water until finally a beautiful calm cool pond caught His sight. As the Linga was not to be placed anywhere before Rameswaram, He looked for someone to keep the Linga while He drank water. 'Lord Kalabhairava', in the form of a small boy, at the request of 'Lord Anjaneya' consented to hold the Linga but only for a short length of time, inconspicuously intended to be shorter than the time in which Lord Anjaneya could get back.

Not a wink later than the stipulated time elapsed did the boy place the Linga down and was no show any longer. Anguished at the boy's carelessness, Lord Anjaneya rushed back and tried to lift the Linga but in vain. After several futile attempts He coiled the Linga with His mighty tail and pulled as hard as he could to which the Linga responded with nothing more than a slight inclination. Then Lord Kalabhairava appeared and expounded to Lord Anjaneya the realities behind the screen.

The Linga here can be seen slightly inclined with horizontal marks around, left by the tail of Lord Anjaneya. The temple tank here with curative powers is watered by a perennial sweet water spring which has fount oblivious in the mountains above. The waters flow into the sacred tank through the mouth of the Holy Bull-mount of Lord Siva, 'Nandi' sculpted beautifully on the side wall of the tank about a foot above the water level which is maintained a constant by the continuous inflow and outflow of the spring waters which replenish the tank with outbreak. The spring water is used for drinking and the water flowing out of the tank is used for irrigation in and around the place.

There are busses to Ramagiri from Uthukottai and Pichattoor which are enroute to Tirupati from Chennai.

Suruttappalli: About 2 km from Uthukottai, near the Andhra Pradesh-Tamil Nadu border and 12 km from Nagalapuram, the ancient temple on the banks of the sizzling Arani river, dedicated to Lord Siva, has a unique feature.

In almost all South Indian temples dedicated to Lord Siva, the Lord is seen in His usual Linga form whereas here at Suruttappalli He manifests in a majestic human form in a reposing posture in His right, mighty, merciful palm. A crown is also seen on His head. Goddess Parvathi, the consort of Lord Siva and other deities are also seen in the 'Sanctum-Sanctorum'.

The legend states that Lord Siva here, took a brief rest after consuming the deluge of deadly poison that emerged from the ocean while it was churned for Amurdha, in order to save the living beings on the whole of Earth, who would otherwise have been killed by the poison.

It is said that this is the only temple all over India where Lord Siva can be seen in this form and in this posture. This historic unique temple is also rich in architecture and comes under the maintenance of the 'Tirumala Tirupati Devasthanam'.

Kalyani Dam: About 18 km from Tirupati, this beautiful dam regulates the outflow of sizzling waters from the resplendent reservoir which takes care of the drinking water supply of the town Tirupati.

Kailasanadhakona: About 43 km from Tirupati, an off-shoot from the main road between Puthur and Vadamalpet leads to this picturesque section of the magnificent Nagiri hills, with a ravishing waterfalls which courses along the huge mountains inheriting all the wholesome goodness of minerals and enrichments the mighty mountains offer. Hence, this water is believed to have curative properties. This place is rapidly developing into a picnic spot.

Horsley Hills: If some one visiting Tirupati in the hot season is looking for a respite

from the scorching sun, here is one. This beautiful summer resort and hill station which had been camouflaged until W.D. Horsley discovered it in 1870 is situated along the mighty ranges of eastern ghats, about 150 km from Tirupati by road via Madanapalle. The last stretch of 10 km, making a difference of 746 m in height between the point and the base,

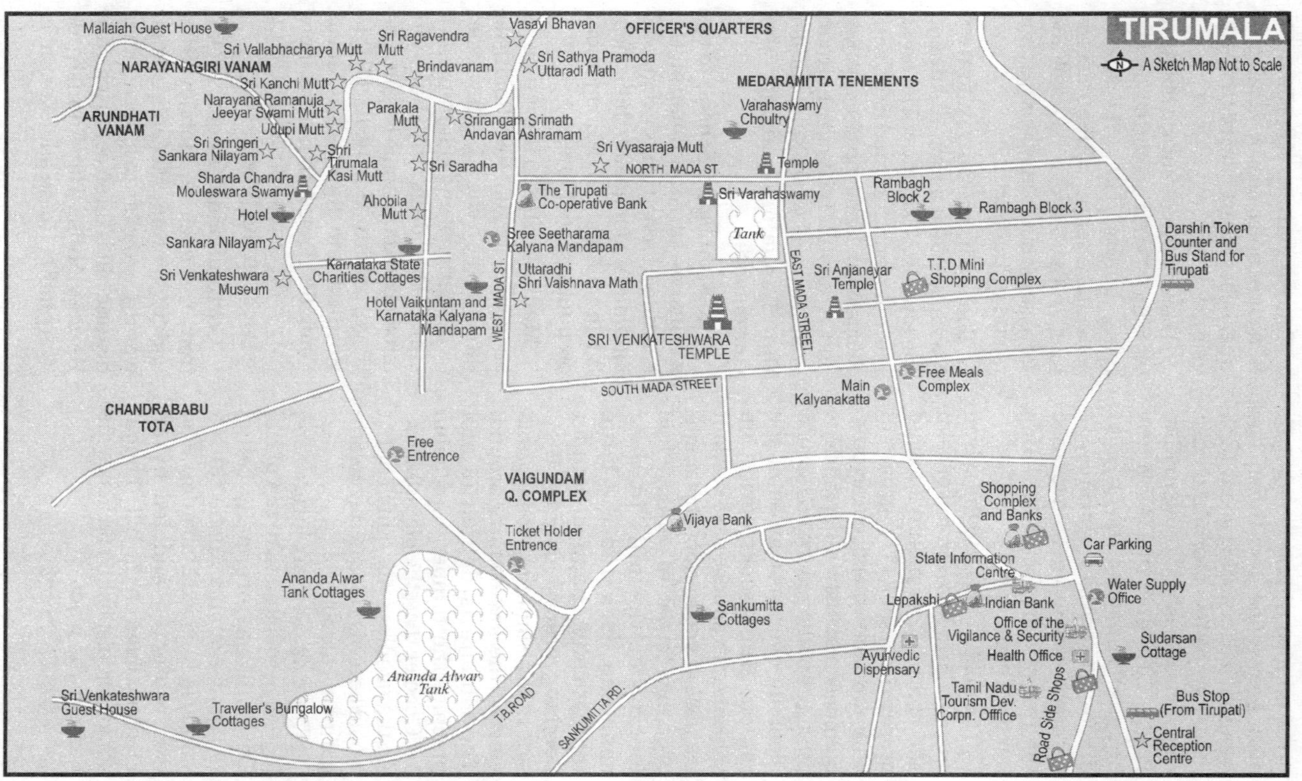
TIRUMALA
A Sketch Map Not to Scale
Mallaiah Guest House
Sri Vallabhacharya Mutt
Sri Ragavendra Mutt
Vasavi Bhavan
OFFICER'S QUARTERS
NARAYANAGIRI VANAM
Brindavanam
Sri Sathya Pramoda Uttaradi Math
Sri Kanchi Mutt
MEDARAMITTA TENEMENTS
ARUNDHATI VANAM
Narayana Ramanuja Jeeyar Swami Mutt
Parakala Mutt
Srirangam Srimath Andavan Ashramam
Varahaswamy Choultry
Udupi Mutt
Sri Sringeri Sankara Nilayam
Shri Tirumala Kasi Mutt
Sri Vyasaraja Mutt
Sri Saradha
NORTH MADA ST.
Temple
Sharda Chandra Mouleswara Swamy
The Tirupati Co-operative Bank
Sri Varahaswamy
Rambagh Block 2
Rambagh Block 3
Ahobila Mutt
Hotel
Sree Seetharama Kalyana Mandapam
Tank
Sankara Nilayam
Darshin Token Counter and Bus Stand for Tirupati
Karnataka State Charities Cottages
Uttaradhi Shri Vaishnava Math
Sri Anjaneyar Temple
T.T.D Mini Shopping Complex
Sri Venkateshwara Museum
EAST MADA STREET
Hotel Vaikuntam and Karnataka Kalyana Mandapam
WEST MADA ST.
SRI VENKATESHWARA TEMPLE
Free Meals Complex
SOUTH MADA STREET
Main Kalyanakatta
CHANDRABABU TOTA
Free Entrence
VAIGUNDAM Q. COMPLEX
Shopping Complex and Banks
Vijaya Bank
Ticket Holder Entrence
Car Parking
State Information Centre
Ananda Alwar Tank Cottages
Water Supply Office
Lepakshi
Indian Bank
Sankumitta Cottages
Office of the Vigilance & Security
Sudarsan Cottage
Health Office
Ayurvedic Dispensary
Ananda Alwar Tank
Tamil Nadu Tourism Dev. Corpn. Offfice
Bus Stop (From Tirupati)
Sri Venkateshwara Guest House
Traveller's Bungalow Cottages
T.B.ROAD
SANKUMITTA RD.
Road Side Shops
Central Reception Centre

gives an idea of how steep it is, even before one gets there. The beautiful hills reaching about 1265 m above sea level form the most elevated table land is south Andhra Pradesh. Here, in this resort, the houses constructed by its discoverer W.D. Horsley, a European civil servant, have stood the test of time for more than a hundred years now.

The mighty hills and the sylvan surroundings here are full of calm and charm. Cool mountain wind graces the region. The groves of teak, red sandalwood, eucalyptus, gulmohar and many other precious produces of the mountains spread gleefully over vast areas of the region. Huge rocks spring up sporadically amidst vast verdant expanse of vegetation. One might probably forget to wink, while looking at the hills in their changing hues and the large fantastically shapped boulder perching precariously on their sides. The summit gives a grand view of the low country around. The climate is delightful and bracing, the temperature being 18^{0}C cooler than the plains below. As the evenings are quite chill, it would be a wise idea to carry warm garments along.

There is also an interesting legend associated with the place. This hill was originally called *Enugu Mallamma Konda* since a saintly lady called Mallamma who was protected and fed by an Elephant lived on the hill. 'Enugu' stands for 'elephant' and hence the name to the place.

Tourists can also visit Horsley's Bungalow and a nearby eucalyptus tree, believed to be more than 100 years old.

There are two vantage points to view the beauties of the landscape lying below. There is also a sericulture centre with numerous birds and a variety of blossoms and three small but sumptuous gardens to add to the mirth.

The nearest railway station Madanapalle is about 40 km and the town is 27 km away. However, this hill resort has road links with Bengalooru, Madanapalle, Chennai and Tirupati. The nearest airport is at Tirupati while some prefer the Bangalore airport for convenience.

The Rishi Valley School: In the extensive surroundings of the exciting Horsley Hills, about 16 km from Madanapalle, this school is run by American Management on public school lines.

Madanapalle: This place is known for its sublime climate all through the year. This has been an educational and cultural centre since the days of the ever remembered Dr. Annie Besant. The Government Hospital, M.L.L. Hospital and Rajkumari Amrut Kaur, T.B. Research Centre, here carry on with their untiring services to the people.

Gurramkonda: About 17 km from the exciting Horsley Hills and 32 km from Madanapalle on way to Cuddapah, this, yet another historic hill is often confused with Horsley Hills. The English for 'Gurram' is Horse and 'Konda' is

Hill and hence 'Gurram Konda' a Telugu nomenclature can be literally put as 'Horse Hill' and not 'Horsley Hill'. A wonderful fort atop the hill offers fascinating views of the low lying area. The 'Rangini Mahal' here was the headquarters of the Governor of 'Tipu Sultan' whose name is perpetuated in history, among a number of traits, for his undaunted resistance to the British.

Sompalle: About 37 km from Horsley hills and 50 km from Madanapalle, this beautiful place and its importance can be traced back to the historic Vijayanagara period. The temple here is one of those ancient ones where the grandeur of the Vijayanagara architecture is unfolded. Another temple in the proximity abounds in excellent rock carvings. A soaring monolithic pillar in front of the temple measures upto 46 m in height. The Kalyanamandapam carved out of stone is another attraction.

Arogyavanam: The Union Mission T.B. Sanatorium here is noted for its yeoman service to the suffering lot. It is an asylum to the T.B. struck patients who walk in down-cast and walk out up and about. A 'Post-Graduate Diploma' course in T.B. is also conducted here.

Kanipakkam: About 10 km north of Chittoor, this place is sanctified by a number of ancient temples. The temples reveal the grandeur of the elegant Chola architecture. The temple dedicated to Lord Vinayaka who is always worshipped as the primary deity in all religious rituals and festivals of the Hindus, celebrates a grand festival for seven days before and after 'Vinayakachathurthi Festival'.

The rulers of the Vijayanagara dynasty and the later ones have also made additions to the number of temples of the region.

Thalakona: Thalakona is a forest located 30-km from Tirupati. Deep in these forests is a 6m perennial waterfall known as 'Talakona'. It is an enchanting picnic spot of great scenic beauty.

Horsley Hills: Horsley hills, situated at an altitude of 1,265m is a hill resort located 151-km from Tirupati and named after WD Horsley, who was the collector of Cuddapah district. Horsley chose this spot for his summer residence. The place is luxuriously green and cool, with a maximum summer temperature of 32°C, and minimum of 20°C.

Accommodation

Tirupati (STD : 08574)

- **Hotel Bliss (3 Star)**
  Near Railway Overbridge,
  Renigunta Road,
  Tirupati - 517 501.
  ☎: 2221650, Fax: 2229514
  E-mail:hotelbliss@hot.bot.com
- **Hotel Guestline Days (3 Star)**
  14-37, Karakambadi Road,
  P.O. Box No. 9,
  Tirupati - 517 507.
  ☎: 2280800/2280366
  Fax: 2227774
- **Hotel Mayura (3 Star)**
  209, T.P. Area,
  Tirupati - 517 501.
  ☎: 2225925, 2225291
  Fax: 2225911

- **Bhimas Deluxe Hotel**
  34-38, G. Car Street,
  Near Railway Station,
  Tirupati - 517 501.
  ☎: 2225521, Fax: 2225471
- **Hotel Bhimas Paradise**
  33-37, Renigunta Road,
  Tirupati - 517 501.
  ☎: 2237271-76, Fax: 2237277
- **Tirumala Residency Hotels**
  Besides Railway Over Bridge
  Renigunta Rd, Tirupati - 1.
- **Kalyan Residency (3 Star)**
  P.No. 177 T.P. Area,
  Tirupati - 517501.
  ☎: (877) 2259780
  Fax: (877) 2259757
  Email: srinivas@kalyanresidency.com
- **Hotel Sindhuri Park (3 Star)**
  19-1-118, 119, T.P Area,
  Tirupati - 517501.
  ☎: (877) 2256430
  Fax: (877) 2256438
  Email: hotelsindhuri@rediffmail.com
- **Hotel Quality Inn Bliss (3 Star)**
  Near Ramanuja Circle,
  Renigunta Road ,
  Tirupati - 517501.
  ☎: (877) 2237770-76
  Fax: (877) 2237774
  Email: blisstpt@vsnl.com
- **Sudalagunda Hotels**
  209, T P Area, Renigunta Road,
  Tirupati - 517501.
  ☎: (877) 2225251/2225666/2225911/2225118/19/21

East Godavari

This beautiful district derives its name from the marvellous river *Godavari* which nourishes many parts of the state with its benevolent waters. This river originates on the Western Ghats at Thriyambakam near Nasik in Maharashtra and takes a long course of 1450 km before meeting its destination, the Bay of Bengal.

This beautiful district is in the northeastern part of Andhra Pradesh. Its district headquarters is Kakinada.The District boundaries are Vishakapatnam, West Godavari, Khammam Districts and Bay of Bengal. The District is known as rice bowl of Andhra Pradesh with lush paddy fields and coconut groves. It is also known as another Kerala. East Godavari is well connected through Rail, Road, Water and Air. The National Highway 5 connecting Chennai and Howrah passes through this district. Rajahmundry and Samarlakota are the railway junctions in the district. The Chennai to Howrah rail line also passes through this district. The district has an airport at Madhurapudi(Rajahmundry Rural), which is 10 km from Rajahmundry and 65 km from Kakinada. There are regular flights from Rajahmundry to Hyderabad, Chennai, Vijayawada etc. Kakinada has sea port which is predicted to be a potentially important port after Chennai, Paradip and Vishakapatnam along the east coast of India.

There are also numerous ancient temples where grand architectural styles unique to certain region or dynasty and a fusion of the styles of two or more regions or dynasties are unfolded. The sculptures of these temples are of genuine excellence. The stone carvings and rock edicts on the walls of the temples recount a number of awesome events, conventions, customs, practices and legends. A number of royal dynasties have bequeathed in the form of architecture and sculptures myriad monuments of perpetual wonder. These ancient monuments have been revered and treasured generations after generations. The temples make very popular pilgrim destinations. The regions or the city around the temples assume festive colour when thousands of devotees congregate during the periodical festivals. Thus tourism is a brisk activity in the region.

Rajahmundry: About 581 km by rail from Chennai, on the way to Calcutta, this historic place is of religious importance. Rajahmundry ideally falls on the beautiful banks of the resplendent river Godavari. Overseeing the river are the ancient temples dedicated to Lords Markandeya and Kotilingeswara. This is a famous pilgrim spot.

Legend has it that 'Markandeya' was born to a devout couple after long pleading prayers to Lord Siva who made an offer to them to choose between a sagacious son with a short span of life and a nitwit with of course a long life while they wisely enough settled for the former. Then the Lord granted them their wish and Markandeya who was supposed to live only for 16 years was born. Markandeya as a child was absorbed in his devotion to Lord Siva. The Lord was pleased with his impeccable austerity. When the time came after 16 years, 'Lord Yama', the God responsible for death appeared before Markandeya to take away his life. Frightened, the boy embraced the 'Sivalinga' in unshakable faith when 'Lord Yama' threw one end of His 'fatal' rope with the other end in His firm grip as it always is, in an attempt to encircle the boy while rope fell around Markandeya and the Sivalinga. Anguished, the Lord blazed in before Yama kicking Him away with His Holy foot. Then Lord Siva was pacified when Lord Yama pleaded He was trying to do just what He was supposed to do. Lord Siva, then, not only pardoned Lord Yama but also declared that the benedicted child Markandeya will remain 16 years of age forever. Thus Markandeya became an immortal.

Rajamundry is also a centre for the manufacture of carpets and sandalwood articles.

Amalapuram: This place is blessed with lush fields, coconut groves, green palms and is criss - crossed by small canals and is really a feast to nature lovers. Located approx. 65 Km from Kakinada via Yanam, this picturesque village offers easy access to other places of tourist interest also.

Annavaram: The ancient temple here forms the crown of the beautiful hill known as 'Ratnagiri' on the banks of the serene river Pampa. This temple is dedicated to Lord 'Veeravenkata Sathyanarayana Swamy' one of the various forms of 'Lord Vishnu'. By a traditional convention devotees undertake a special vow and perform regular poojas in praise of the Lord here and get their wishes granted.

At an estimated average, about one lakh devotees undertake vow and offer 'Poojas' every year, most of whom are couples. This temple is much opted by many for conducting marriages and the Holy thread ceremony of the Brahmin community. The important annual festivals are Bhishma Ekadasi and Kalyanotsavam in January-February and Vysakha Ekadasi in April-May. It is a sacred piligrim centre on a hill top known as Ratnagiri at a distance of 72 kms from Rajahmundry. The presiding deity at Annavaram is Veeravenkata Satyanarayana Swamy. The main temple resembles a chariot with four wheels. It is believed when Vrata is performed in the name of Satyanarayana Swamy by devotees, their wishes will be fulfilled. It is estimated on an average about one lakh Vratas are performed here every year by couples generally.

Antarvedi : Antarvedi is 10 km from Narasapur by boat and 24km from Razole by road. The Shrine of Sri 'Lakshminarasimhaswami' at this place is of religious importance. The Lakshmi-narasimhaswami Kalyanam celebrated on the Bhishma Ekadasi day during January-February is attended by thousands of pilgrims.

A fair is also held and lakhs of people attend the celebrations. Devotees come here to have a holy dip in the 'Sapta Sagara Sangama Pradesam' (the confluence of the sea and the 'Vasishta Godavari', one of the seven branches of Godavari), as it is believed that all their sins will be washed away by a single dip in the holy river.

Adurru : Adurru is located near Nagaram in Razole Taluk of East Godavari district. The village lies on the West bank of the Vainetaya, a branch of Godavari river 9.5 Km from the sea.The mound is locally known as Dubaraju Gudi. Archaeological Survey of India conducted excavations in 1953 and brought to light, remains of stupas, Chaityas and Vinaras among which the Mahastupa, built on wheel shaped plan 17 feet in diameter with a raised platform running all around the drum and Ayaka platforms on cardinal directions. The Buddhist remnants spread across an area of approximately 2.04 acres.Adurru is located 30 Kms from Amalapuram and is well connected by Road. The nearest Railway Station is Rajahmundry and distance is 130 Kms from it and by Air from Hyderabad, Vizag Airports.

Bikkavolu : Bikkavolu is located in the East Godavari district of Andhra Pradesh where a group of six fine temples exist. The Bikkavolu temples though not included in the pancharamas, form the earliest group and typical examples of the Dravidian style of architecture in the heart of coastal Andhra. The three temples located on the outskirts of the Bikkavolu village form the early group, with cognate architectural features and the other temples located within the village belong to a later group.

Yanam : This is a part of the Union Territory of Puducherry lies on the spot where the Coringa river and Godavari river separate. The total area of the region is 30 sq. km. Being an important trade centre and port town, Yanam is connected by road with all the major towns nearby like Kakinada, Rajamundri and Vishakhapatnam.

Papikonda: The 'Bison Range' here flaunts some bewitching sights. It is spread in three districts, viz : Khammam, East Godavari and West Godavari The picturesque hills soar at places to a height of 2,280 m above sea level aptly punctuated by gorgeous gorges in between. The benevolent expanse of the verdant forests provides land to vast plantations of teak and bamboo. The mighty mountains contiguous to the ravishing river, open out and close in to form enclosures which give rise to placid little lakes. The delirious scenery leaves a lasting picture of awesome delight in the minds of the visitors.

Draksharamam: This sacred place situated 17 km from Kakinada and 40 km from Rajahmundry has an ancient

tranquil temple dedicated to Lord Siva. 'Sapta Godavari Kundam' or 'Seven Godavari Tank' is the sacred temple tank situated near the temple. The legend has an interesting event as to the naming of the tank.

The magnificent river Godavari known as the Akhanda Godavari or 'unbranched Godavari' was divided into seven smaller rivers here by the 'Sapta Maharishis' or 'Seven Sages' in order to attain the objective of their severe penance. Three of those seven divisions, the Bharadhwaja, the Viswamithra and the Jamadagni are submerged underground.

According to another legend, a king by name Daksha Prajapathi who had been bestowed upon with the coveted divine honour of being the father-in-law of the Almighty Lord Siva, as the Lord had married the King's daughter Dakshayani who was indeed none but a human incarnation of Goddess Parvathi, disdained out of vanity to invite his son-in-law to the 'Mahayagna' a religious ritual which he performed extending cordial invitations to all others. While Goddess Parvathi attended the Yagna though without invitation, in an attempt to straighten up the strained relationship between the father-in-law and the son-in-law, She too was ill-treated. Unable to bear the insult, She subjected herself to self-immolation. Thus the place came to be known as '*Daksha Vatika*' which in due course of time transformed into '*Dhraksharamam*' which is the present name.

The grand architecture and sculpture in the temple is the result of Chalukya and Chola styles a number of ancient 'Sasanas' or edicts can be seen engraved on the walls. The famous Telugu poet Srinatha who lived in the 4th century is said to have written the famous Bhimakhanada, an epic on this Holy place.

It is also believed that sage Vyasa performed a penance here and called the place '*Dakshina Kasi*' or 'Southern Banares'. Pilgrims from far and wide throng the temple during the Sivarathri festival.

The art form 'Veeranatyam' is very famous here. It is believed this place is where Lord Veerabadra was created by Lord Siva out of His Jata-Jhuta, Holy hair.

Ryali: About 25 km from Rajahmundry, this wonderful temple where the presiding deity is Sri Jaganmohinikesava Swamy, unravels excellent sculptures, marvellous architecture and rare iconographs.

Papikonda Sanctuary: Spread over an area of 591 sq.km, the

sanctuary is situated along the

slopes of Papikonda range. Many animals including tiger and birds are seen here.

Coringa Wildlife Sanctuary: A sanctuary of 235 sq.km was established in 1978. It is in the Godavari delta. Fishing cats, crocodiles, otters and many water birds are seen here.

Accommodation

Rajahmundry (STD : 0883)

- **Anand Regency (3 Star)**
  26-3-7, Jampeta,
  Rajahmundry - 533 103.
  ☎: 2461201 (4 lines),
  4655401 (6 lines)
  Fax: 2461204
- **Dwaraka Hotel**
  Dwarka Hotel Fort Gate,
  Rajahmundry - 533 105.
  ☎: 2471851-53.
- **Kalpalatha Lodge**
  Devi Chowk
  Rajahmundry - 533 104
  ☎: 2475669
- **Hotel Vasant Mahal**
  G. N. T Road, Eluru - 534 006.
  ☎: (8812) 2230090/2231088/
  2231080-82
- **Metro Lodge**
  RTC Complex
  Morumpadi Junction
  Rajahmundry - 533 103.
  ☎: 2467183
- **Ramesh Guest House**
  Near Fort Gate, Mochi Street,
  Rajahmundry - 533 104.
  ☎: 2478074
- **South India Lodge**
  Near Fort Gate, Main Road,
  Rajahmundry - 533 101.
  ☎: 2436261

Sri Jaganmohinikesava Swamy Temple - Ryali

West Godavari

This district has enormous potential for Tourism because of its location of religious Monuments/Temples and rich historical or archaeological heritage. It is richly cultivated land and major crops are rice, sugar-cane, coconut and to some extent cotton & tobacco. The headquarters is the town of Eluru. The places of religious temples/ institutions and historical/ archaeological significance in the district are presented briefly hereunder:

Bhimavaram: The place is noted for a big Naturopathic Hospital located in an extensive garden. Of the several temples at the place, Bhimeswara and Someswara are important. The Sivalingam in the temple of Bhimeswara is said to be Swayambhu Lingam (Self manifested). Located 107 km from Vijayawada and 272 km from Vishakapatnam, Gunupudi Bhi mavaram is also well known for the temple Soma Rama, which is considered as one of the Pancharama temples. The face of Shiva lingam in this temple is called Sadyojathamukha Swaroopam. Mass marriages (especially during Shivarathri) are being conducted at this temple premesis. The local people say that couple getting married at this Pancharama place have a peaceful understanding life. Sri Someswara Janardhana swamy temple, which is also considered as one of the Pancharama Kshetras is situated here.

Dwaraka Tirumala: Located about 40 Km from Eluru, this place is of Hindu religious importance owing to the temple of Lord Venkateswara which is also known as "ChinnaTirupati" locally.

Pallakollu: Formerly known as Palakota and Palakolanu, this place is situated about 10 Km from Narasapur. The Kshira Ramalingeswara Temple which is one of the Pancharamas is an important pilgrim center. This coastal town is an important trading town. This is the birth place of Padmasri Allu Ramalingaiah. U. Srinivas, a world renowned exponent of Mandolin, was born here.

Pattisam (Pattiseema): It is one of the ancient and sacred places in South India located 120 km from Elluru and 40 km from Rajamundry. The religious importance is due to the shrines of Veerabhadra and Bhavanarayana situated on the Devakuta Parvatam overlooking the Papi Hills in the heart of River Gowthami.

Penugonda: It is Mandal Headquarter. This place is believed to be the birthplace of Kanyakaparameswari, the goddess of the Vaisyas. The temple of Kanyakaparameswari is the most important religious institution in the town.

Pedavegi: Pedavegi originally known as Vengi. The Capital of the

Salankayanas, Vishnukundins and the East Chalukyas and was a flourishing city at the time of Satavahanas. It is a petty village now with a few visible landmarks.

Khandavalli: This very ancient village situated on the banks of Vasista Godavari is at a distance of 12 Km from Tanuku. It is also known as panchalingakshetram owing to the existance of five Sivalingams in the temple of Markandeswara-Mrukandeswara . This strange phenomena of five lingams in a temple is found only at Benarus and Rajahmundry. Hence this place is considered to be of religious importance.

Tanuku: Tanuku is the Headquarters of the Mandal and it is said to be the birthplace of Adikavi Nannaya Bhattaraka, who undertook the translation into telugu of Mahabharatha written in Sanskrit by Sage Vedavyasa.

Kolleru Lake: This enchanting expanse of serene waters which caters to the drinking water requirements of the region has long since been an irresistable invitation to the rare pelican birds and the humans alike. These fascinating birds have made this place an ideal ground for them to nest and procreate. This exotic flock of birds in a picturesque environ is obviously greeted by flocks and flocks of tourists. Mention to this fascinating lake can be found in the writings of the famous Bernier who visited the court of the Mughal emperor, Shahjahan and also toured the entire country including the Golconda Kingdom.

Guntupalli: About 44 km from Eluru and 85 km from Vijayawada, Guntupalli in the western parts of the Godavari district reveals the Buddhist monuments of the olden days. The rock cut caves in the awesome hills, the placid environs and the ancient images of Buddha, Stupas and Viharas render tranquility.

Narasapur: Located 128 km from Eluru, this place is famous for Sri Adi Kesava Emberumanar Swamy temple, which is a sacred pilgrimage destination for the vaishnavites.

Accommodation

Bhimavaram (STD : 8816)

- **Sri Thay Residency A/C**
  P.P. Road,
  Bhimavaram - 534 202.
  ☎: 236645
- **Surya Residency**
  Bhimavaram - 524 201.
  ☎: 222363
- **Hotel Rajkamal**
  25-59, Main Road, Tanuku,
  West Godavari - 534 211.
  ☎: (8819) 2224965-69
- **Hotel Sudha**
  Juvvalapalem,
  Bhimavaram - 534 201.
  ☎: 222486.
- **Hotel Ratnam**
  Railway Station Road,
  Bhimavaram,
  West Godavari - 534 202.
  ☎: (8816) 2223765/2224370-74

Krishna

This is another magnificent river, the other one being Godavari, by the name of which a district is known. Krishna has its founts in the robust ranges of the mighty Western Ghats, Mahabaleshwar in the state of Maharashtra. It has a beautiful long course of 1290 km and mingles with the Bay of Bengal. The main tributary of this resplendent river is the ravishing river Tungabadra. Obviously both the rivers are revered as sacred as all rivers and waterways in the nation. All along the benign banks of this beautiful path of serene waters are situated lush green fertile landscape and many ancient cities which retain their pristine beauty even with the foray of modernisation.

The beautiful, ancient and important city of Vijayawada with its scenic hills, historic monuments and sacred pilgrim centres is ideally situated on the beautiful banks of Krishna. The temples and hills have historic and Puranic references. The legends allude the regions here had been the stage of many mythical happenings. There is also a monument built after Mahatma Gandhi.

In and Around Vijayawada

Kanaka Durga Temple: This ancient temple in the beautiful city adds divine significance to the picturesque hill the 'Indrakila'. Goddess 'Kanaka Durga', the presiding deity here manifests in a four foot tall idol with eight mighty arms all holding frightening weapons to destroy the evil. Mahishasura, the demon king can be seen under the Holy feet of the Goddess with Her 'Trident' ripping apart his heart. The Goddess who ravages the demon turns benign and benevolent to the innumerable devotees who have reposed unshakable faith in Her. Every bit of the rich precious jewellery and the beautiful fragrant flowers and festoons seems to emulate one another in adoring the all merciful Goddess.

The temple management has earmarked three points for devotees to have 'Darshan'. The first one is inside the Sanctum-Sanctorum in close quarters to the deity, the second one just outside the Sanctum-Sanctorum and the third, a little further away. 'Lakshakumkum' Archana, a special ritual is part of every day activities. The chanting of 'Manthras', the phrases praising the Goddess and the divine music buoy up the devotees to the higher realms of spirituality.

Legend has it that it was on this Holy hill 'Indrakila', Arjuna, the invincible archer of the great epic 'The Mahabharatha' performed a severe penance and obtained the sacred 'Pasupathasthra' from Lord Siva who appeared in the form of a hunter to test Arjuna's bravery and commitment to the cause and after He was pleased, bestowed upon Arjuna the wish he sought. Hence, this hill also has a temple in which Lord Siva manifests as a hunter.

Visiting Hours: 4:30 - 22:30 (Kanaka Durga Temple)

Archana Hours: 4:30 hrs, 8:00 hrs, 14:00 hrs and 18:00 hrs

The Gandhi Hill: In the heart of the city of Vijayawada, this is a fabulous monument dedicated to the 'Father of the Nation'. A memorial library and a seminar hall can be seen here. Various figures representing cottage industries which the Mahatma had laid repeated emphasis upon, are beautifully reflected on the crimson marbles. Identical images of his house at his birth place Porbandar, his Phoenix Ashram in South Africa, Sabarmathi Ashram at Ahmedabad all along the lavish incline of the hill are vociferous of the austere life style of the Mahatma.

A modest planetarium can also be found here. The observatory here has a telescope and a camera through which the curious visitors peep into the wonders of the firmament.

Kuchipudi: Kuchipudi in this district is where the gorgeous dance form originated and permeated to every nook and corner of the nation. This dance finds a warm welcome in many a festival, cultural meet, public function and marriage. The place Kuchipudi continues to play patron to the sought-after dance form through its Government run institution. At the mention of the name 'Kuchipudi' what springs

to the mind is the ancient classical dance which evolved right at this place, 60 km from Vijayawada. 'Siddendra Yogi', a forerunner who has contributed in leaps and bounds to this divine dance was born here. This dance has a wide acclaim and forms an indispensable part of many a cultural meet.

The place also has a Government run institution, 'Natyacharya' which offers a five year dance course leading to a degree. Aspirants with a keen bent of mind for the fine art are taught and trained and shaped into wonderful dancers, here.

Kondapallee: Kondapalle is where the inspiring toys, dolls and puppets made out of wood originate. It is chiefly a cottage industry practiced by a particular community which migrated from Rajasthan. These articles replete with splendid workmanship adorn the interiors of several homes. The sleightful hands behind their making are worth a million felicitations. Prosaic pieces of a special wood are vivified at the crafty hands of these doll-makers who seem to bring out these marvellous articles with effortless case, quite reticent of the skill and labour it warrants.

Different parts of the ethereal toys, made separately, are glued together to form a single astounding specimen. This craft is chiefly practiced by a community which is believed to have migrated from Rajasthan fleeing their homes during the Moghul invasions. The gorgeous variety of the dolls includes mythical figures, humans, animals, birds, plants, fruits, temples, houses, carts and a host of fictitious figures. This place is about 20 km from Vijayawada.

Maginapudi Beach: About 11 km from Machilipatnam, this beautiful beach which offers copious enchantment to the visitors has also the pride of being part of a historic city. Maginapudi has apparently served more than one purpose in the olden days. Not only as an important commercial centre but as the point of dispersal to various other points of India too, was the city of Maginapudi known for. The beach has a natural bay, comparatively shallow and hence safe waters. To compliment the natural beauty, there are man-made fountains in a conscientiously laid park.

Accommodation is avialable at Machilipatnam. The nearest railway station, Machilipatnam is about 15 km away. The nearest airport which is about 85 km away is at Vijayawada. Maginapudi can also be reached by road from Vijayawada after a 85 km drive.

Ghantasala: About 21 km west of Machilipatnam and 280 km from Hyderabad, Ghantasala, the excavation site has yielded evidence to reckon it as one of the places where Buddhism flourished. The Buddhist stupa unearthed here has a unique design. 12 constellations of zodiac can be seen engraved on the brick cube set in the centre. Ghantasala can be reached from places like Srikakulam, Vijayawada and Vishakapatnam by Government run busses. Accommodations are available at Vijayawada.

The Victoria Jubilee Museum: The Museum of the Archaeological Department situated on Bundar Road contains sculptures and painting. Pre historic materials, such as stone tools, microliths and neolithic implements are also on display. There is a colossal granite statue of the Buddha and also a well preserved standing white limestone figure of the Buddha from Alluru, dating from the 3rd century - 4th century. Opens at 1030 to 1700. Friday holiday. Entry - free. For camera - Rs.5.

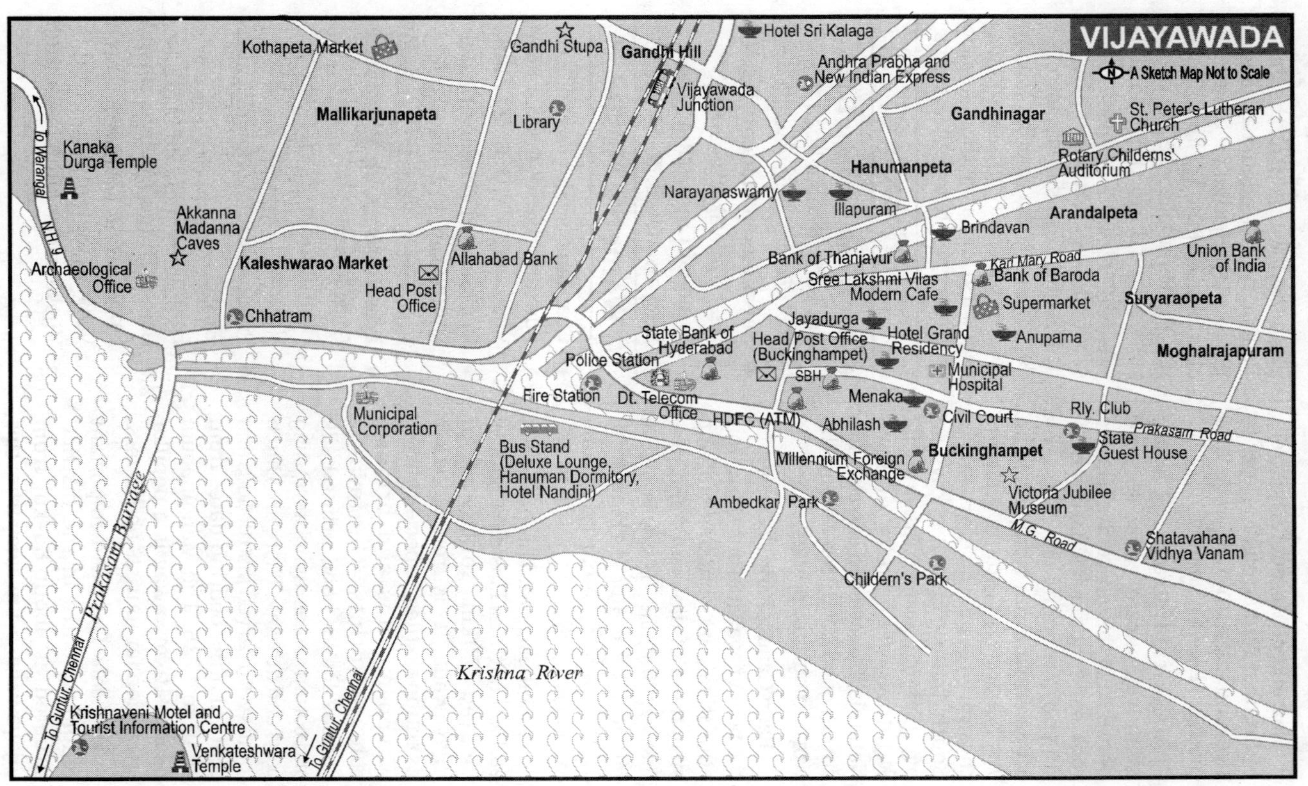
VIJAYAWADA
A Sketch Map Not to Scale
Kothapeta Market
Gandhi Stupa
Gandhi Hill
Hotel Sri Kalaga
Andhra Prabha and New Indian Express
Vijayawada Junction
Mallikarjunapeta
Library
Gandhinagar
St. Peter's Lutheran Church
Rotary Childerns' Auditorium
To Warangal
Kanaka Durga Temple
NH 9
Hanumanpeta
Narayanaswamy
Illapuram
Arandalpeta
Akkanna Madanna Caves
Brindavan
Union Bank of India
Archaeological Office
Kaleshwarao Market
Allahabad Bank
Bank of Thanjavur
Karl Mary Road
Bank of Baroda
Head Post Office
Sree Lakshmi Vilas Modern Cafe
Supermarket
Suryaraopeta
Chhatram
Jayadurga
State Bank of Hyderabad
Head Post Office (Buckinghampet)
Hotel Grand Residency
Anupama
Moghalrajapuram
Police Station
SBH
Municipal Hospital
Fire Station
Dt. Telecom Office
Menaka
Civil Court
Rly. Club
Municipal Corporation
HDFC (ATM)
Abhilash
Prakasam Road
State Guest House
Bus Stand (Deluxe Lounge, Hanuman Dormitory, Hotel Nandini)
Millennium Foreign Exchange
Buckinghampet
Victoria Jubilee Museum
Ambedkar Park
M.G. Road
Shatavahana Vidhya Vanam
Prakasam Barrage
Childern's Park
Krishna River
To Guntur, Chennai
Krishnaveni Motel and Tourist Information Centre
Venkateshwara Temple
To Guntur, Chennai

Hazrathbal Mosque: A holy relic of Prophet Mohammad is kept in the mosque in the city and displayed once a year.

Mogalrajapuram Caves: Mogalrajapuram caves located 3km east of the city centre has five rock cut sanctuaries dating back to the 7th century AD. The Mogalarajapuram temple has an 'Ardhanarisvara' statue which is thought to be the earliest in South India. Cave 2 shows an overhanging cornice with artificial windows. The idols of Lord Nataraja, Vinayaka in one cave are still in good condition among the worn images of deities.

Rajiv Gandhi Park: Located near the new Vijayawada bus stand, this educative park contains built-up structures of dinosaurs and pre-historic animals. There is also a Musical Fountain working from 7.30 p.m. to 8.15 p.m. closed on Mondays.

Machilipatnam: This port town earlier known as Masulipatnam, is located 70km southeast of Vijayawada. It is renowned for its cotton textiles, especially finely woven muslins and brightly coloured prints. The town is famous for its hand printed silk and cotton sarees, upholstery, sling bags and dresses. There are Dutch tombs with carved instructions and coats of arms bearing dates from 1649 to 1725. The Manginapudi Beach, 10kms away is a popular attraction for tourists and divers.

Hamsala Devi: An important religious centre in the district, situated at about 85-km from Vijayawada. 5-km away from this place the Krishna joins the Bay of Bengal. It is considered as a sacred place of pilgrimage being the confluence of the Krishna and the sea. The Shrine of Venugopalaswami, constructed during the rule of the Chola Kings, is an important place of worship. A festival celebrated in honour of this deity for eight days from Magha Suddha Navami to Bahula Padyami (January-February) attracts thousands of pilgrims even from other states.

Hostels

- **Annapurna Students Home**
  Sai Baba Temple Road,
  RTC Colony, Vijayawada - 8.
- **Savaniketan Student Hostel**
  Near Vinayaka Theatre,
  Srinagar Colony, Ring Road,
  Vijayawada - 8. ☎: 2544280

Women's Hostel

- **Chandana**
  Punnamathotha, Bundar Road,
  Vijayawada - 10. ☎: 2474995
- **Krishnaveni Womens Hostel**
  KVR Street, Krishna Nagar,
  Vijayawada - 10. ☎: 2482889
- **Preethi Working Womens & Girls hostel**
  Chuttugunta, Eluru Road,
  Vijayawada - 4. ☎: 2432101
- **Priyadarshani Working Womens Hostel**
  Patamata, Vijayawada - 6.
- **Sri Sai Durga Womens Hostel**
  Opp. Gayatri Complex,
  Vasavya Nagar,
  Vijayawada - 10. ☎: 2483126

Accommodation

Vijayawada (STD : 0866)

- **Hotel Ilapuram (3 Star)**
  Besant Road, Gandhi Nagar,
  Vijayawada - 520 003.
  ☎: 2571282 (10 lines)
  Fax: 2575251
  E-mail: hotelilapuram@com
- **Hotel Kandhari International (3 Star)**
  M.G. Road, Labbipet,
  Vijayawada - 520 010.
  ☎: 2471310 (10 lines)
- **Hotel Mamata (3 Star)**
  Eluru Road, Vijayawada - 2.
  ☎: 2571251, Fax: 2574373
- **Hotel Manorama (3 Star)**
  27-38-61, M.G. Road,
  Vijayawada - 520 002.
  ☎: 2572626, 2577221
  Fax: 2575619
- **Hotel Raj Towers (3 Star)**
  Congress Office Road,
  Governorpet, Vijayawada - 2.
  ☎: 2571311 (10 lines)
  Fax: 2571317
- **Quality Inn Dv Manor (3 Star)**
  M.G. Road, Vijayawada - 10.
  ☎: 2474455, Fax: 2483170
  E-mail: dvmanor@hotmail.com
- **Sree Lakshmi Vilas Modern Cafe**
  Besant Road, Governorpet,
  Vijayawada - 520 002.
  ☎: 2572525 (5 lines)
- **Hotel Krishna Residency**
  Rajagopalachari Street,
  Governorpet,
  Vijayawada - 520 002.
  ☎: 275301-2,274709
- **Abhinava Hotel,**
  Kaleswara Rao Road,
  Governorpet, Vijayawada - 2.
  ☎: 2431495
- **Adarsh Boarding & Lodging**
  BRP Road, Vijayawada - 1.
  ☎: 2567802
- **Ajantha Hotel**
  Eluru Road, Vijayawada - 2.
  ☎: 2572341
- **Alfa Hotel & Lodging**
  Panja Centre, Vijayawada - 1.
- **Anil Rest House**
  Governorpet, Vijayawada - 2.
  ☎: 2577723
- **Annapurna Hotel**
  Tadankivari St, Governorpet,
  Vijayawada - 2. ☎: 2571245
- **Archana Hotel**
  Besant Road, Governorpet,
  Vijayawada - 2. ☎: 2577864
- **Bharani Lodge**
  Poornanandampet,
  Vijayawada - 3. ☎: 2573853
- **Bombay Guest House**
  Congress Office Road,
  Governorpet, Vijayawada - 2.
  ☎: 2572357
- **Divya Rest House**
  Havaldar Lane,
  Near Post Office,
  Vijayawada - 1. ☎: 2424723
- **Durga Vilas Lodge**
  Peddibotlavari Street,
  Governorpet, Vijayawada - 2.
  ☎: 2576698

- **Dwaraka Rest House**
  Railway Station Road,
  Wynchipet, Vijayawada-1
- **Eskimo Lodge**
  Gandhinagar, Vijayawada - 3.
  ☎: 2578332
- **Guru Guest House**
  Prakasam Road, Vijayawada - 2.
  ☎: 2576093
- **Guru Hotel**
  Gandhinagar, Vijayawada - 3.
  ☎: 2572879
- **Hotel Abhilash**
  Gudavallivari Street,
  Governorpet, Vijayawada - 2.
  ☎: 2577711
- **Hotel Adhikari**
  Bunder Road, Vijayawada - 10.
  ☎: 2472402
- **Hotel Anupama**
  Kaleswara Rao Road,
  Governorpet, Vijayawada - 2.
  ☎: 2571224
- **Hotel Apsara**
  Rajaji Street, Governorpet,
  Vijayawada - 2. ☎: 2573743
- **Hotel Ashoka**
  Gopalareddy Road,
  Governorpet, Vijayawada - 2.
  ☎: 2573121
- **Hotel Chandra**
  Purnanandampet,
  Vijayawada - 3. ☎: 2571211
- **Hotel Chaya,**
  Sivalayam Street,
  Governorpet, Vijayawada - 2.
  ☎: 2576336
- **Hotel Jagapathi International**
  Gandhinagar, Vijayawada - 3.
  ☎: 2571291
- **Hotel Janasudha Lodge**
  Gandhinagar, Vijayawada - 3.
  ☎: 2574598
- **Hotel Mamata**
  Opp. Old Bus Stand,
  Eluru Road, Vijayawada - 2.
  ☎: 2571251/2572858
- **Hotel Manorama**
  Old Bus Stand Bunder Road,
  Vijayawada - 2. ☎: 2571621
- **Hotel Menaka**
  Near Old LIC Office Besant Road,
  Governorpet, Vijayawada - 2.
  ☎: 2574117
- **Hotel Modern Cafe,**
  Besant Road, Vijayawada - 2.
  ☎: 2432825
- **Hotel Monika Lodge**
  Behind Police Control Room,
  Governorpet, Vijayawada - 2.
  ☎: 2571334
- **Hotel Narayana Swamy**
  Hanumanpet, Vijayawada - 2.
  ☎: 2571221
- **Hotel Navayuga**
  Mandapativari Street,
  Bunder Road, Vijayawada - 2.
  ☎: 2574141/2575229
- **Hotel Paradise**
  Congress office Road,
  Governorpet, Vijayawada - 2.
  ☎: 2576403
- **Hotel Pecso**
  Peddibotlavari Street,
  Governorpet, Vijayawada - 2.
  ☎: 2571206/2571207
- **Hotel Prashanth**
  Kandulavari Street,
  Vijayawada - 1. ☎: 2422535

- **Hotel Sangeetha**
Bunder Road, Vijayawada - 10.
☎: 2471266
- **Hotel Santhi**
Near Apsara Theatre,
Governorpet, Vijayawada - 2.
☎: 2577351
- **Hotel Santosh**
JD Hospital Road,
Governorpet, Vijayawada - 2.
☎: 2572714/2573215
- **Hotel Saranant**
Bunder Road, Vijayawada - 2.
- **Hotel Sarovar**
Rajagopalachari Street,
Governorpet, Vijayawada - 2.
☎: 2 575255/2572824
- **Hotel Shirdi**
Bunder Road, Vijayawada - 2.
☎: 2571266
- **Hotel Shirisha**
Bodemma Hotel Centre,
BRP Road, Vijayawada - 1.
☎: 2564204
- **Hotel Siddartha**
Kaleswara Rao Road,
Governorpet, Vijayawada - 2.
☎: 2571261
- **Hotel Sree Surya**
Museum Road, Governorpet,
Vijayawada - 2. ☎: 2574401
- **Hotel Sreenivasa**
Behind UTI Office,
Governorpet, Vijayawada - 2.
☎: 2573337/2573338
- **Hotel Sri Balaji,**
Besant Road, Governorpet,
Vijayawada - 2. ☎: 2572146
- **Hotel Sri Vijaya Durga Bhavan**
Gopalareddy Road,
Governorpet, Vijayawada - 2.
☎: 2576720
- **Hotel Supriya**
Opp.Autonagar Gate,
Bunder Road, Vijayawada - 7.
- **Hotel Swamy**
peddibotlavari Street,
Governorpet, Vijayawada - 2.
☎: 2577214
- **Hotel Swapna Lodge**
Durgiah Street,
Governorpet, Vijayawada - 2.
☎: 2575386/2573172
- **Hotel Tilothama**
Near Old Bus Stand,
Governorpet, Vijayawada - 2.
☎: 2572103/2574201
- **Hotel Vikram**
Purnanandam pet,
Vijayawada - 3. ☎: 2571321
- **Jaya lodge**
Governorpet, Vijayawada - 2.
- **Kanakadurga Rest House**
Kandulavari Street,
Vijayawada - 1. ☎: 2421148
- **Komala Vilas**
Kothapet, Vijayawada - 1.
☎: 2566286
- **Krishna Boarding & Lodge**
Samarangam Chowk,
Vijayawada - 1. ☎: 2564194
- **Lakshmi Brindavan Lodge**
Besant Road, Vijayawada - 2.
☎: 2572580
- **Mayuri Rest House**
Wynchipet, Vijayawada - 1.
☎: 2563310
- **Meghdoot Hotel**
JD Hospital Road,
Governorpet, Vijayawada - 2.
☎: 2577598
- **Menaka lodge & Jyothi lodge**
Governorpet, Vijayawada - 2.
☎: 2565208

- **Modern Cafe Lodging**
  Samarangam Chowk,
  Vijayawada - 1. ☎: 2422535
- **Nayagara Rest House**
  Bunder Road, Vijayawada - 2.
  ☎: 2573484
- **New Adarsh Boarding & Lodging**
  BRP Road, Vijayawada - 1.
  ☎: 2567802
- **OM Merchant's Lodge**
  Kothapet, Vijayawada - 1.
  ☎: 2562281
- **Prasant Lodge**
  Near Railway Station,
  BRP Road, Vijayawada - 1.
  ☎: 2567129
- **Ramakrishna Rest House**
  Governorpet, Vijayawada - 2.
  ☎: 2571071
- **Roja Rest House**
  Near Ramakrishna Theatre,
  Patamata, Vijayawada - 6.
- **Sree Nivas Bunder Road, Governorpet, Vijayawada - 2.**
  ☎: 2573337/2573338
- **Sri Durga lodge**
  Prakasam Road,
  Governorpet, Vijayawada - 2.
  ☎: 2430474
- **Sri Hotel Annapoorna**
  Besant Road, Governorpet,
  Vijayawada - 2. ☎: 2577162
- **Sri Krishna Rest House**
  Near Kothagullu,
  Seshaiah Street,
  Vijayawada - 1. ☎: 2424114
- **Sri Lekha Lodge**
  Tadankivari Street,
  Governorpet,
  Vijayawada - 2. ☎: 2571275
- **Sri Sai Deluxe Lodge**
  Achutaramaiah Street,
  Hanumanpet,
  Vijayawada - 3. ☎: 2577640
- **Sri Sailaja Rest House**
  Wynchipet, Vijayawada - 1.
  ☎: 2564717
- **Srinu Hotel**
  Seshaiah Street,
  Vijayawada - 1. ☎: 2425751
- **Sujamal Lodge,**
  Bhavanipuram,
  Vijayawada - 12. ☎: 2412437
- **Suryabhavan Lodge**
  Ramgopal Street,
  Vijayawada - 1. ☎: 2424165
- **Tourist Home**
  Prakasam Road, Governorpet,
  Vijayawada - 2. ☎: 2578330
- **Welcome Hotel**
  Gandhinagar, Vijayawada - 3.
  ☎: 2573286
- **Krishna Residency (3 Star)**
  Rajagopalachari Road,
  Governorpet, Vijayawada - 2.
  ☎: 2572709/2571571/2573197/2575301/02
  Fax: 2574373
- **Hotel Vikram (3 Star)**
  16-10-50, P Swamy Street,
  Poornanandampet,
  Vijayawada - 3. ☎: 2571321-25
- **Lalitha Hotels**
  26-13-72, Sanyasi Raju street,
  Gangar, Vijayawada - 3.
  ☎: 2571291-5
- **Thilotthama Hotels**
  52-1/8-4, Near Siddhartha
  Medical College,
  Vijayawada - 8.
  ☎: 2572103/2572204/2574201/2576202/2573203/5/6/9

Ananthapur

This district of Andhra Pradesh encapsulates many historic monuments, pilgrim spots and also several modern developments. The ancient forts and temples speak volumes of the splendid architecture and wonderful sculpture. Most of the citadels and forts unravel the grandness and intricacies of the Vijayanagara Empire. These forts encapsulate a number of forts with in and have been built to be self-consistent. Water sources can also be found in some forts. The rugged fort walls have protected the inmates against many fierce battles for long periods. However, in the late part of history some of them have been conquered, saboteured and the treasures inside, ravaged by the invaders.

The *Prasanthinilayam* at Puttaparthi, the Holy abode of Bhagavan Sri Sathya Sai Baba, is a Heaven on Earth. A number of devotees from all over the world throng the tranquil place. The trust run by Bhagavan Sri Sathya Sai Baba is actively engaged in a number of services to the cause of humanity. The trust run hospital, equipped with state-of-the-art technologies renders free medical service to the deserving and the desolate. The drinking water project put up by the trust quenches the thirst of the entire disrict including the dry areas which would otherwise be drought-hit most often. The educational institutions which have attained varsity status, moulds young minds and sparks the creative thinking ability of the brain.

The district also has a place to flaunt, which has entered the coveted '*Guinness Book of World Records*'. It was in 1989 that the 550 year old tree 'Thimmama Marrimanu' ambled into the record book for being the biggest and oldest of its kind. The ancient tree also commands religious reverence.

Ananthapur is thus a region of diverse importance. There are places and monuments which recount historic and prehistoric events. The architecture and sculpture has reached great heights. The beautiful idols at Hemavathi Temple, made out of translucent stones produce musical chime when dabbed. Tourists of varied tastes find interests to suit their own.

Puttaparthi: This place about 30 km from Dharmavaram and 250 km from Bangalore is sanctified by Bhagavan Sri Sathya Sai Baba. Born in Puttaparthi, Sri Sai Baba is believed to be the reincarnation of Shirdi Sri Sai Baba. Even as a child, Sri Sai Baba displayed sagacity and profound wisdom and amused His playmates with His paranormal powers. As days rolled into weeks and weeks into months and months into years, His power of aura wafted over a very wide region spreading His fame all over the nation and abroad. Devotees flocked to Him in millions and in just a hand's turn he relieved them of their unsurmountable woes. The number of His followers is constantly on the rise. His devotees make a broad variety right from the meek to the opulent. A weekly 'Bhajan' which is the group recital of devotional songs, hymns and verses in praise of Bhagavan Sri Sathya Sai and all other forms of God is customary among His devotees.

'Prasanthinilayam', as it is called, His abode is one of the sacred places where tranquility prevails. The name literally means 'abode of peace'. The tranquility, serene atmosphere, subtle silence are all too compelling for any one to leave the place. In short, it is a Heaven on Earth.

The 'Sathya Sai Baba Trust' whose principal philosophy is 'Service to Humanity is Service to Divinity' renders untiring services to the very cause of humanity through a variety of its institutions, hospitals and projects. The entire Ananthapur district owes innumerable thanks to the trust for its drinking water project which caters to the sweet-water needs of its people. Even the dry belt areas of the disrict are supplied with sufficient water. The hospital run by the trust has specialist doctors, experts, famous surgeons and also advanced medical equipments which incorporate state-of-the-art technology. What is indeed touching about the hospital is that it offers free service to the desolate and the deserving regardless of religion, caste or creed.

The educational institution here has attained varsity status. It has a unique curriculum which includes special subjects in spirituality, meditation, discipline and impeccable character are imparted as a way of life here. The education received here opens up new creative arenas in the exploring brains of the inquisitive individuals.

The museum on a nearby hillock has models of the Golden Temple of Amritsar, the Holy Mosque at Mecca, etc. The models of these monuments which are the places of worship of people of varied religions corroborate the unity of human race above all diversities.

The planetarium within the premises of the Holy Prasanthi-nilayam is yet another addition to the attractions here. The planetarium virtually rockets the viewers to the unknown parameters of the mysterious universe.

Lepakshi: Located in between Hindupur and Kodikonda checkpost, about 16 km from the railway station at Hindupur, the beautiful small village Lepakshi has an ancient temple dedicated to Lord Siva. The murals of this temple recount episodes from the life of devotees and Saints. Diverse forms of God can also be seen. Every inch of the temple is an architectural splendour. The grand Vijayanagara style is vivid on the ornate workmanship.

There are references to this temple in 'Skandapuranam' which puts it as one of the 108 exclusive temples dedicated to Lord Siva. Sri Virupanna who was the treasurer at the Penukonda fort of the Vijayanagara empire was instrumental in raising this temple where Lord Siva manifests in the form of Lord Veerabadra.

An astounding feature in this temple is the 'Antarikshastambham' which is indeed a hanging pillar suspended from the roof. The sculptures, pictures and paintings command felicitations to their makers. A gigantic monolithic 'Nandi', the Holy Bull-mount of Lord Siva, measuring 6 ft in height and 8 ft in length, is the biggest of its kind.

The sacred place is obviously an active pilgrim centre. Asvayujamasam, a 10-day long annual festival highlighted by the temple chariot celebrations draws scores of devotees from far and wide. This occurs in the month of February every year. Comfortable accommodations are available for the tourists.

Penukonda : Here the magnificent fort in the backdrop of a mighty hill which raises to a height of 914 m has been the target of many a historic foray. The ancient inscriptions refer to this fort as 'Ghangari'. The fort today encapsulates the remains of an awesome number of ancient precious monuments some of which have been partly and others completely destroyed by a number of attacks. It is said that there were as many as 365 temples inside the fort. These places of worship and other monuments were ravaged and plundered by the invading Muslim rulers. The remains of these ancient treasures are vociferous of the pain caused by the ruthless destruction meted out to them.

Thimmamma Marrimanu: A place which strikes a strange

triangular significance, as a place of religious importance, as a place of picnic and also as a place which has quite justifiably occupied the pages of Guinness Book of World Records is Thimmamma Marrimanu.

It is believed that the huge tree here is named after 'Thimmamma' a saintly woman who was aptly deified by the local populace. The belief also holds that if childless couple worship 'Thimmamma' they would immediately be blessed with a child. The big 'Jatara' conducted during 'Sivarathri' festival attracts thousands of devotees.

Even picnic makers cannot help fancying the spot for its sheer beauty and the grandness of the huge tree whose age is estimated around 550 years.

This ancient living biological treasure entered the coveted book of Guinness World Records in the year 1989 as the biggest tree with 1100 prop roots. It is about 35 km from Kadiri.

Gooty : One of the oldest citadels of Andhra is situated here. About 45 km from Ananthapur this ancient fort has been in place right from the period of Ashoka to the later British, changing numerous hands in the meanwhile. This mammoth fort resembles a shell in its composure and has 15 parts with 15 gates. A prudent master-plan behind its construction is explicit from the way it has been designed to be self-dependent in all respects including sources of water.

Rayadurg : The fort here is yet another masterpiece of the Vijayanagara empire. The fort ideally located at an altitude of 2727 ft above sea level has many interior forts. The layout and design of these magnificent structures have been so skilfully planned to keep the enemies at bay. There is also a wonderful temple known as 'Dasabhuja Ganapathi Temple' dedicated to Lord Ganapathi.

Here, the principal deity in all Hindu endeavours, Lord Ganapathi manifests with 10 shoulders which is discernable from the name 'Dasabhuja' which means '10 Shoulders'. The Holy image, about 4 m in height, has been sculpted out of single stone.

This fort, about 90 km from Ananthapur, very much in Andhra, is in fact closer to Bellary of the adjacent state Karnataka, which is only 25 km away.

Hemavathi: About 10 km from Amarapuram and 25 km from Madakasira and with Kodikonda on the east, this historic village which was prominent between the 8th and the 10th century AD under the Nolamba Pallavas is where stands the ancient Siva temple where Lord Siva manifests in the form of 'Lord Doddeswara'. The town known as 'Henjeri' during the Pallava reign was later rechristened as Hemavathi. The temple structure is a standing evidence of an ancient architectural excellence. It leaves one in sheer astonishment if one purports to fathom out the hard, meticulous and ethereal workmanship the sculptors of yore should have summoned to bring out such extraordinary sculptures. Amazing more, is the fact that nature had endowed them with such exotic, hard-found rocks, for the idols here are stunningly transparent and produce pleasant metal-like sound when dabbed. 'Rajendra Chola' had probably been so fascinated by the massive pillars with intricate carvings that he had removed as many as 44 of them to adorn the temple at Thiruvedi, which is evident from the inscriptions.

Captivating carvings can be found on the low roof made out of a large stone. A gigantic 'Nandi', the holy bull-mount of Lord Siva, at the ingress measures 8 ft in length and 4 ft in height. The temple wall reflects exquisitely carved human figures while the ornate carvings on the pillars in

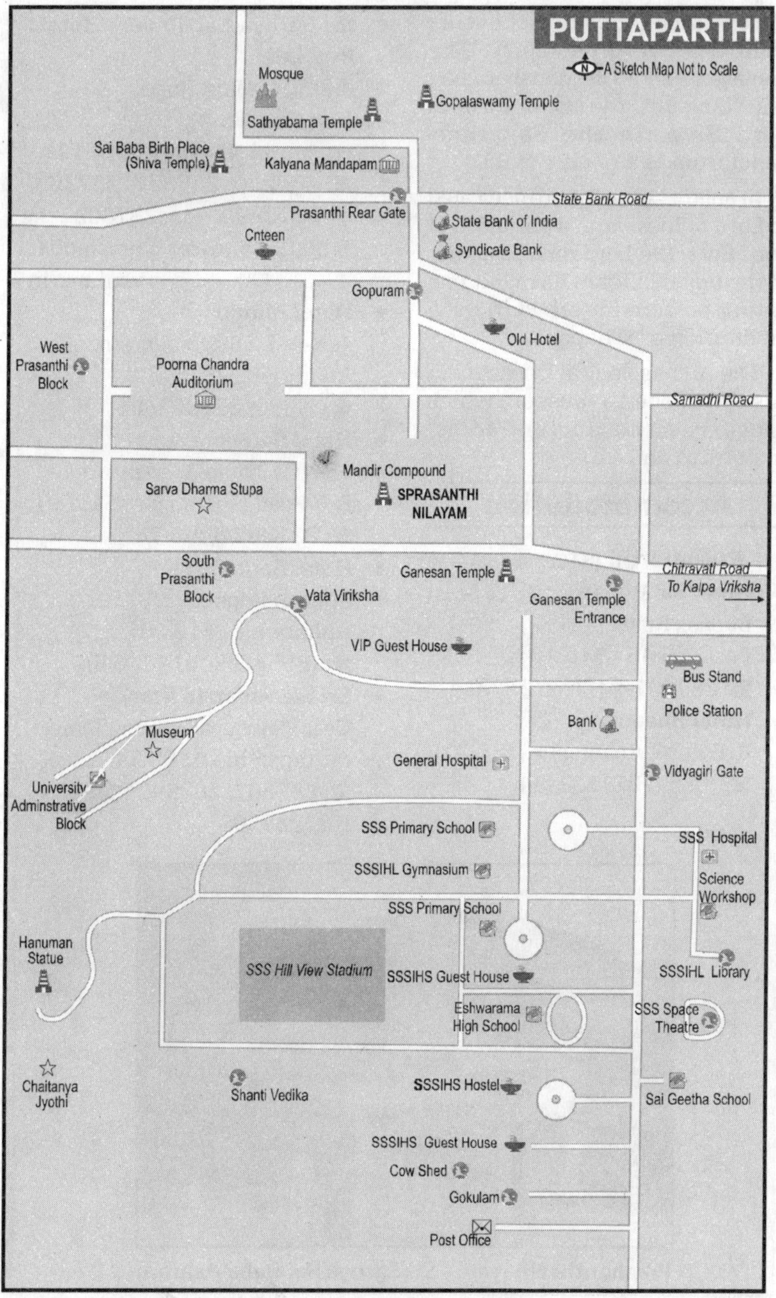
PUTTAPARTHI
N
A Sketch Map Not to Scale
Mosque
Gopalaswamy Temple
Sathyabama Temple
Sai Baba Birth Place
(Shiva Temple)
Kalyana Mandapam
State Bank Road
Prasanthi Rear Gate
State Bank of India
Cnteen
Syndicate Bank
Gopuram
Old Hotel
West
Prasanthi
Block
Poorna Chandra
Auditorium
Samadhi Road
Mandir Compound
Sarva Dharma Stupa
SPRASANTHI
NILAYAM
South
Prasanthi
Block
Ganesan Temple
Chitravati Road
To Kalpa Vriksha
Vata Viriksha
Ganesan Temple
Entrance
VIP Guest House
Bus Stand
Police Station
Bank
Museum
General Hospital
Vidyagiri Gate
University
Adminstrative
Block
SSS Primary School
SSS Hospital
SSSIHL Gymnasium
Science
Workshop
SSS Primary School
Hanuman
Statue
SSS Hill View Stadium
SSSIHS Guest House
SSSIHL Library
Eshwarama
High School
SSS Space
Theatre
Chaitanya
Jyothi
Shanti Vedika
SSSIHS Hostel
Sai Geetha School
SSSIHS Guest House
Cow Shed
Gokulam
Post Office

the enclosed porch depict events from the two great epics 'The Ramayana' and 'The Mahabaratha'. The 'Lingam', the usual form of Lord Siva, in the Sanctum-Sanctorum is a good 6 ft tall.

In another temple here dedicated to Lord Siddeswara, a variation of Lord Siva, the Lord manifests not in the usual Lingam form but in a sitting posture absorbed in deep meditation or 'Thapas'.

The Archaeological Department has established a museum which preserves the ancient idols, sculptures and carvings.

Accommodation

Puttaparthi (STD : 08555)

- **Hotel Sai Renaissance (2 Star)**
  Bypass Road,
  Puttaparthi - 515 134.
  ☎: 287591-94, Fax: 287324
- **Hotel Bheema**
  R. F. Road, Anantapur - 515 001.
  ☎: (8554) 221531-34
- **Sri Sathya Sai Towers Hotels Pvt. Ltd.**
  2,3/604, Main Road,
  Post Box No. 2,
  Prasanthi Nilayam - 515 134.
  ☎: 287270, 287327, 287368, 287329 Fax: 287302
  E-mail: saitower@giasblg01.vsnl.net.in
- **Hotel Manju**
  428-1-3, Dharmavaram,
  Anantapur - 515 672.
  ☎: (8559) 222303/4/5
- **Hotel Sampoorna**
  15-442, kamalanagar,
  R. F. Road, Anantapur - 515 001.
  ☎: 221852/3/4/6/7/8
- **Hotel Saptagiri**
  Subash Nagar,
  Anantapur - 515 001.
  ☎: (8554) 220914/5/6/8/9
- **Sri Sai Sadan (2 Star)**
  Near Venugopalaswamy Temple,
  Puttaparthi - 515 134.
  ☎: 287507, 287890/91/92
  Fax: 287508

Prashanthi Nilayam - Sri Sathya Sai Baba Ashram

Warangal

This district of Andhra is glutted with ancient temples, historic monuments and massive forts. Archaeologists find a bounty here while the layman is awe-struck. Historians have a lot to take note of. The archive of the district appeals to historians while the monuments attract archaeologists. The Kakatiya rulers have contributed in leaps and bounds to the glory of the region. The Warangal Fort built by the Kakatiya ruler Ganapathi Deva is a fine example of construction in ingenuity as beyond the forbidding moat all along the outer periphery. There are two walls, the outer one built of mud whereas the inner one composed of rugged stone.

The temple of 'thousand pillars' where each one of them is embellished with conscientious carvings is an ancient specimen of architectural excellence. The Badrakali Temple atop a picturesque hill again reflects the grandeur of Chalukya architecture. The Ramappa Temple reveals what a great connoisseur of art and architecture its constructor had been. Konalupaka had been under the regime of Chalukyas and Cholas as evidenced from the chronicles. A Jain temple here is believed to have been built 2000 years ago.

Since the entire region had been in the middle of many historic events, which is learnt from the monuments and read from the inscriptions, the State Department of Archaeology and Museums has carefully collected these ancient treasures in and around Konalupaka and preserved them in a museum in a chronological order. The museum is open to visitors.

In and Around Warangal

Warangal Fort: This massive fort built by the Kakatiya ruler Ganapathi Deva and his daughter Rudramma is one of the masterpieces of the 13th century. The fort consists of two walls, the sturdy inner one built of stone and the outer one of mud. The fort is also surrounded by moat to offer additional protection. Excellent sculpture and exquisite carvings adorn the remains of the four magnificent gateways built of stone. The ruins provide an insight into the grand workmanship of a marvellous structure.

Thousand Pillar Temple: This ancient temple which stands in ruins now is a telling example of

the grandeur of the Kakatiya architecture of the Chalukya rulers. Built in 1163 by Rudra Deva this star-shaped temple comprises 3 shrines, dedicated to Lord Siva, Lord Vishnu and Lord Surya, the

'Sun God'. The temple has a thousand ornately carved pillars. Marvellous sculpture marks the temple all over. The black basalt 'Nandhi', the Holy Bull-mount of Lord Siva is a monolith with a glossy finish. It is a baffling thought that the whole structure with every bit of it intact would look like when even the remnants are so astonishing.

Badhrakali Temple: The famous bhadrakali temple of the Kakatiya period, situated on a hill with a 2.7m tall stone image of the Goddess is the major attraction. Atop a scenic hill between Hanamkonda and the city of Warangal this ancient temple, again an outcome of the splendid Chalukyan architecture, is dedicated to Goddess 'Badhrakali', the Goddess of Bravery. Here the Goddess manifests with eight mighty arms all holding threatening weapons to fight evil and protect the noble.

Pakhal Lake: Another beautiful sheet of placid waters, spreading over 12 sq. miles, situated about 50 km from Hanamkonda, the Pakhal lake is surrounded by picturesque sylvan region on three sides and a bund on the other which in fact is responsible for the formation of the lake itself from a beautiful river. This river coursing over an outcrop of the magnificent Vindhya mountains confronts the bund and thereby forms this enchanting enclosure of water. The lake is suffused with fish and also contains otters and alligators.

Laknavaram Lake: About 70 km from Hanamkonda, this lake is contemporary to the Ramappa lake. Three short bunds across three narrow valleys give rise to this beautiful lake. This artificial lake which looks more natural like the Ramappa lake surrounded by the breathtaking beauties of nature leaves a lasting picture in the minds of the visitors.

Ramappa Temple: About 70 km from Warangal, this ancient temple known as Ramappa temple or Ramalingeswara temple dates back to 1213 AD. The presiding deity of this magnificent temple which proclaims the greatness and glory of the Kakatiya architecture through every inch of its massive structure is Lord Siva. An inscription in the temple holds that this Holy monument of architectural excellence was built by Rudra Swami on behalf of the then ruler Kakati Ganapathy Deva under whom he was the chief commander. It also conveys, the region was called *Ranakude* which is now in Atukaru Province and there were temples of Kateswara, Kameswara and Rudreswara, all the three dedicated to Lord Siva.

The pillars with ornamental workmanship and ornate ceilings display scenes from the two great epics 'The Ramayana' and 'The Mahabaratha'. The icons of several forms of God and Goddess, figures of warriors, acrobats and images of beautiful maiden in various dancing postures are the highlight of the sumptuous sculpture found here. The figures made of black basalt carved to a glossy finish are captivating. Every single specimen of the myriad items found here unravels the kind of connoisseur and patron of art the ruler 'Ganapathi Deva' was.

The serene Ramappa lake which offers pleasant excitement is just one kilometre away.

Vemulawada: About 35 km from Karimnagar, this ancient temple is dedicated to Lord Raja Rajeswara, a variation of Lord Siva. The sacred lake here known as Dharma Gundam is believed to have curative properties. The festivals celebrated are Maha Sivarathri and Kalyanotsavam.

Kolanupaka: This historic place was an active religious centre of Jains and the second capital of Kalyani Chalukyas during the 11th century AD. Historic battles kept the village rolling from the hands of Chalukyas to Cholas and then to Kakatiyas. Owing to a number of reasons the place lost its charm and the Kakatiyas moved their capital to Orugallu near here after developing the place into one fit for the purpose. Now the region abounds in historic monuments, ancient temples, sculptures and paintings of the 10th and the 11th century AD. Kolanupaka is 80 km from Hyderabad.

Jain Temple: The Jain temple here in Kolanupaka contains beautiful images of Thirthankaras. This ancient temple of Saint Mahaveera stands here for 2000 years now. The impressive image of St. Mahaveera is carved entirely out of precious jade.

Sri Veeranarayana Temple: Chalukyan style is reflated on this wonderful temple built around 1104 AD whose countenance allude that it was originally a Jain temple and later converted to the present one dedicated to Lord Vishnu. This is situated in Kolanupaka.

Someswara Temple: This temple at Kolanupaka was constructed by the Kalyani Chalukya emperor Someswara III. Typical Chalukya architecture decorate the structure and the sculpture is a real splendour.

Kolanupaka Site Museum: More than 100 images of the ancient sculptural excellence collected in and around Kolanupaka are displayed in the Museum with a particular emphasis on the grand architecture of the Someswara Temple complex. These monuments recount a great deal from the Chalukyan and the Kakatiyan periods.

Visiting Hours: 10:30 - 17:00 hrs. (No entrance fees)

Eturnagaram Sanctuary: Spread over 812km of dry deciduous mixed forests, this sanctuary homes tigers, leopards, many other animals and birds. Located approx. 80 km from Warangal. The best season to visit this sanctuary is between October and May.

Pakhal Wildlife Sanctuary: In an area of 860sq.km with dry deciduous mixed type forests, many types of animals including tiger, hyena, wild dogs and birds are seen. Located 60 km from Warangal.

Pembarti : Located 60 km from Warangal, Pembarti is famous for the sheet metal art. For the lovers of handicrafts, the town is worth a visit.

Accommodation

Warangal (STD : 08712)

- **Ashoka Hotel Ratna**
  6-1-163, Main Road, Hnk,
  Hanamkonda,
  Warangal - 506 001.
  ☎: 2578491 - 92.
- **City Grand Hotel**
  15-2-64, Rangampet,
  Warangal - 506 007.
  ☎: 2424567 / 87
- **Gouri Shankar Hotel**
  8-6-16, Station Road,
  Warangal - 506 002.
  ☎: 2421382/2421383
  2441834-36
- **Hotel Shanthi Krishna**
  Station Road,
  Warangal - 506 002.
  ☎: 2426607 - 08
- **Hotel Ratna**
  Pochamma Maidan,
  Warangal - 506 012.
  ☎: 2500096/2500555/
  2500645-49
- **Hotel Vijay**
  11-15-24/1, Laxmipura,
  NRM Road, Warangal - 506 013.
  ☎: 2445755
- **Surya Hotel Pvt. Ltd.**
  8-6-16, Warangal - 506 002.
  ☎: 2441834 - 36

Kurnool

This district of Andhra Pradesh is also known for its famous ancient temples and pilgrim centres. '**Mantralayam**' which is popular worldwide is situated here. Saint Sri Raghavendra whose 'Brindavan' is at Mantralayam has devotees in every corner of the world. Tungabadra, the tributary of river Krishna flows by the place. The Brindavan of Sri Raghavendra has been established also in several other parts of India.

Ahobilam is where a cluster of three ancient temples can be seen. One of them is dedicated to 'Lord Narasimha', an incarnation of 'Lord Vishnu' who assumes the unique form of Narasimha with a lion's head and a human body. Here all the nine forms of Lord Narasimha are worshipped. The place is also marked by picturesque hills and scenic surroundings.

The Nallamalai forests with a captivating landscape punctuated by hills and replete with typical sylvan flora and fauna also covers historic and pilgrim spots like Srisailam, Mahanandi, etc. Srisailam apart from being the centre of one of the 12 'Jothirlingas' of Lord Siva is also the place of a fascinating wildlife sanctuary.

The unique 'Nava Brahma Temple' is situated at Alamapuram, the place which abounds in legends - Kurnool has everything to appeal to every visitor of every taste and liking.

In and Around Kurnool

Mantralayam: This sacred place is situated on the sumptuous banks of the splendid river Tungabadra which is a tributary of the magnificent river Krishna. This tranquil place is where Saint Raghavendra, a prominent saint in the holy hierarchical order of 'Sri Madhvacharya', shed His mortal coils. The 'Brindavan' here entombs the mortal remains of the saint. The air is filled with divine serenity here. It is believed that the saint exists in His Holy subtle form after he had relinquished the material world and that He will continue to dwell in this form till the point of time which marks the completion of 700 years from the time he attained 'Jeeva Samathi'.

Saint Sri Raghavendra took the 'Dwaita' philosophy promulgated by Sri Madhvacharya to places beyond horizons. 'Dwaita' the philosophy upheld by the Madhva School of thought is one of the three great philosophies, the other two being 'Advaita' and 'Visishtadvaita' promulgated by the Saivaite Saint Sri Adisankara and the Vaishnavite Saint Sri Ramanuja respectively. Saint Sri Raghavendra is believed to be the reincarnation of 'Prahlada', the divine prodigy who as an ardent devotee of Lord Vishnu even in His childhood displayed extraordinary wisdom, impeccable sagacity and untarnished courage against all odds imposed by his demon father Hiranya whom the all merciful Lord killed assuming the Lion-head and human-body form to rid Prahlada of the turmoils He was faced with.

Sri Raghavendra has a lot of devotees belonging to various castes and creeds far and wide as a result of which a number of 'Brindavans' have been established all over the country. These centres of worship follow the tradition unique to Madhva culture. 'Annadhana' or free meals is provided to the devotees every day at Manthralayam and also at certain other 'Brindavans'.

Mantralayam has road links with all major cities. The nearest railway station 'Mantralayam Road' is 15 km away.

Srisailam: About 232 km south of Hyderabad, on the gorgeous banks of the mighty river Krishna, the ancient city Srisailam has fascinating features.

The Bhramaramba Mallikarjunaswamy Temple, dedicated to Lord Siva stands on a picturesque hill amidst the verdant expanse of Nallamalai forest. This ancient temple is enclosed by mighty and tall fort walls. The 'Linga' here is one of the 12 'Jothirlingas' or the 'Lingas of Fire (Light)' in India.

The temple is also the seat of Mahakali in the form of Bhramaramba. The legend has it that Lord Siva and his consort Goddess Parvathi manifested to 'Lord Nandhi' the sacred bull who performed a penance.

There is a lot more to relish. Within the premises there are other antique shrines which include the Sahasra Linga Temple the Pancha Pandava Temple and the Vatavriksha Temple. The most appealing feature is that the devotees are not prevented from touching the age-old icons and the Holy Feet, an act which they seem to revere as part of worship. Devotees of all caste and creed follow the custom of touching the Holy Feet. The Srikhareswara Swamy Temple is also dedicated to Lord Siva while there is also a temple dedicated to 'Lord Ganesa'.

The Srisailam wildlife sanctuary, part of which falls in Guntur district provides asylum to a large number of rare species. The sylvan region graced by the nonchalantly beautiful creatures attracts visitors from far and wide.

Ahobilam: About 74 km from Nandhyal and 360 km from Hyderabad, the place also known as 'Singavel Kundram' has an ancient temple dedicated to 'Lord Narasimha', one of the incarnations of 'Lord Vishnu' in which the Lord manifests in the form with the head of a Lion and the body of a man to kill the demon-king Hiranya. The interesting feature of this temple is that all the nine forms of Lord Narasimha known as 'Nava Narasimha' are worshipped. The lower Ahobilam is replete with sumptuous sculptures depicting scenes from the ageless epics.

There are also three more shrines not too far-away from one another. One of them forms the sacred crown of the scenic hill while another is situated at the foot of the hill and the third, about 6 km away.

Mahanandi: Situated 320 km from Hyderabad and 16 km from Nandhyal, Mahanandi the divine Bull-mount of Lord Siva is one of the nine exclusive Nandis known as the 'Nava Nandi'. It is ideally nestled in the vast ranges of the scenic Nallamalai hills. The presiding deity here is 'Mahanandeeswara', a manifestation of Lord Siva in the usual 'Lingam' form.

The temple tank is watered by five natural sweet water springs which are astoundingly perennial. The incessant waters from the springs suffice to irrigate 1000 acres of banana plantations.

Accommodation

Kurnool (STD : 08518)

- **Hotel Raja Vihar Delux (3 Star)**
  Bellary Road,
  Kurnool - 518 001.
  ☎: 220702 (10 lines)
  Fax: 225097
- **The Maurya Inn (3 Star)**
  40/304, Bhagyanagar,
  Kurnool - 518 004.
  ☎: 224999 (10 lines)
  Fax: 248990
  E-mail: cybercafe@netsource online.com
- **Bhupal Hotel**
  D.NO.40/383, Park Road,
  Kurnool - 518 001.
  ☎: 222266/226312-16
- **Hotel Jayasree**
  D.NO.40-301, Bellary Road,
  Kurnool - 518 001.
  ☎: 226500/227212-15/
  226961-63

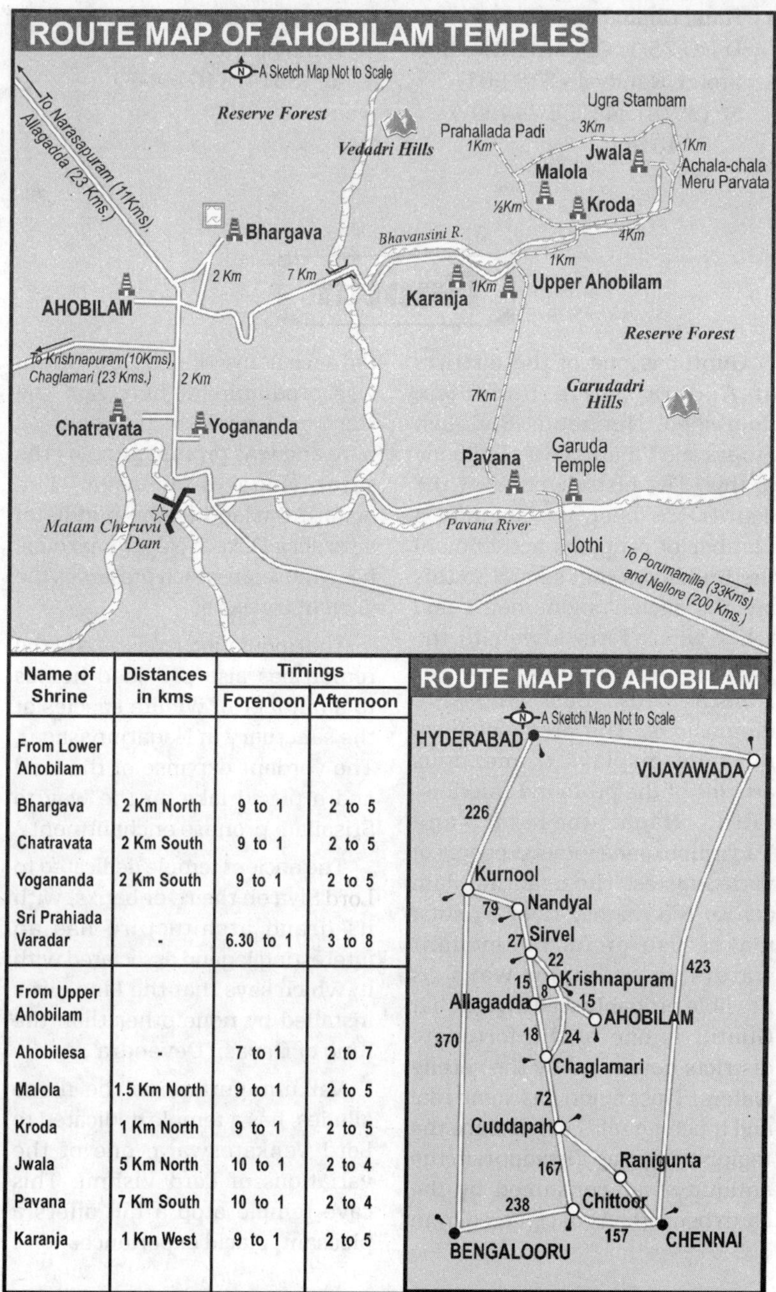

Name of Shrine	Distances in kms	Timings	
		Forenoon	Afternoon
From Lower Ahobilam			
Bhargava	2 Km North	9 to 1	2 to 5
Chatravata	2 Km South	9 to 1	2 to 5
Yogananda	2 Km South	9 to 1	2 to 5
Sri Prahiada Varadar	-	6.30 to 1	3 to 8
From Upper Ahobilam			
Ahobilesa	-	7 to 1	2 to 7
Malola	1.5 Km North	9 to 1	2 to 5
Kroda	1 Km North	9 to 1	2 to 5
Jwala	5 Km North	10 to 1	2 to 4
Pavana	7 Km South	10 to 1	2 to 4
Karanja	1 Km West	9 to 1	2 to 5

- **Hotel Chanakya**
  D.NO.25/1, Opp. APSRTC Bus Stand, Nandyal - 518 501.
  ☎: (8514) 244006/244007/ 244014

- **Hotel Tourist**
  Nandyal - 518 501.
  ☎: (8514) 246494-97

Guntur

Guntur is one of the districts of Andhra where Buddhism flourished. Numerous Buddhist Stupas and Viharas bear testimony to this. The historic cities of the district has been the stage of a number of religious activities of the Buddhism and sequel to this are the ancient monuments and relics which form a weir to the past. The Mahastupa at Amaravathi has massive dimensions. The archaeological museum displays tremendous articles of the profound Buddhist faith. Nagarjunasagar and Nagarjunakonda interest people of varied tastes. The beautiful dam across the mighty river Krishna makes use of its benevolent waters in as many ways as possible probably well aware that Guntur is one of the fortunate districts nourished by the serene waters. This region has some real and touching tales to tell since the region known as Vijayapuri in the antiquity was consumed by the earth beneath. As deciphered from the ancient inscriptions, Buddhism was predominant here and the Mahayana form of Buddhism emerged here and was promulgated by the saint Nagarjunacharya. The beautiful island in the middle of an artificial lake at Nagarjunakonda has a museum which preserves the ancient treasures.

The undulating landscape of the region has also provided homes to a number of widlife species at the sanctuary in Nagarjunasagar. The verdant expanse of the land and a placid lake on the way to Srisailam promise enchantment.

The ancient temple dedicated to Lord Siva on the river banks, with its grand architecture has an interesting legend associated with it, which says that the Linga was installed by none other than the King of Devas, 'Devendra'.

Vaikuntapuram, as the name alludes, has a temple dedicated to Lord Venkateswara, one of the variations of Lord Vishnu. This cave temple atop a hill offers a pleasant, placid experience.

In and Around Guntur

Amaravathi: About 35 km west of Guntur, this historical place Amaravathi situated on the sumptuous banks of the splendid river Krishna, contiguous to Dhanyakataka, the ancient capital of the mighty Satavahana rulers is replete with evidence to show that it was once one of the platforms of the wide-spread Buddhism. Over two thousand years ago, a Holy Buddhist Stupa stood here overlooking the magnificent river Krishna on its north, measuring about 36.5 ft across and about 29 m in height. The stupa built of special bricks baked in kiln, faced with glossy slabs made of marbles brandishes enviable carvings displaying events from the sublime life of Buddha along the crown of its rotunda and either sides of the railing. Amaravathi is hence, a famous pilgrim centre of the Buddhists.

Amaravathi can be reached by road from Guntur, Vijayawada or Hyderabad which are about 35, 82 and 350 kms respectively. The railway stations at Guntur and Vijayawada are 36 and 82 kms away. The Vijayawada airport is 65 km from Amaravathi. Excellent accommodations are available at Guntur and Vijayawada.

Sri Amareswara Swamy Temple: This ancient temple dedicated to Lord Siva stands on the extensive banks of the enchanting river Krishna. Legend has it that the 'Linga' the usual form of Lord Siva was installed by 'Lord Devendra' the head of 'Devas', at the end of 'Dwapara-yugam' one of the four cyclic periods of time, in the order of millions of years.

Archaeological Museum: The fascinating museum at Amaravathi houses extraordinary sculptures. Among the treasured ancient sculptures are the lotus medallions, lotus-carved cross-bars of railings, panels depicting Jataka tales, the revered 'Bodhi' tree and devotees in front of it in the act of worship, Dharma-chakras and numerous other figures. These relief medallions are fine examples of the gorgeous Indian art. These splendid sculptures span over a long period of time from 200 BC to 250 AD. The Amaravathi School of Art whose products have been taken to Sri Lanka and parts of South-east Asia is marked with a distinction like the Mathura and Gandhara arts.

Vaikuntapuram: About 5 km from Amaravathi a tranquil cave-temple on a beautiful hill is dedicated to Lord Venkateswara, the presiding deity of the temple at Tirumala Tirupati in Chittoor district. The legends say that Lord Venkateswara mani-fested here. 'Vaikuntam' is the Holy abode of the Lord who is a variation of Lord Vishnu and hence the place came to be known as 'Vaikuntapuram'. Recital of Rosary and performance of Pujas is carried out everyday.

Nagarjunasagar / Nagarjunakonda: 'Nagarjunasagar' a beautiful dam across the mighty river Krishna set in picturesque environs serves more purpose than one. This enchanting dam site is the favourite resort of scores of tourists.

'Vijayapuri', the ancient name of the place, the old capital of Ikshvaku Empire nurtured a grand Buddhist civilization as long back as the 3rd century AD. Natural calamities had then buried them alive underground. The initial excavations carried out in 1926 led to more and more as fascinating relics, Mahachaita, the sacred Buddhist stupa, the ramshackle remains of a once sturdy university, vihara, Buddhist Monasteries which had been the sacred abode of many a Monk, 'Aswamedha' the sacred altar on which oblations were offered, exciting prehistoric tools which corroborate ancient ingenuity and the reticent ruins of a number of grand ancient monuments were unearthed. A Brahmi inscription states that the Mahachaita, the sacred stupa encapsulates the holy relics of Lord Buddha.

Nagarjunakonda, a serene island amidst the placid waters of a beautiful artificial lake preserved in a museum, these excavated ageless treasures. It is also learnt that the ancient town was the seat of Mahayana Buddhism, one of the two forms of Buddhism in which Buddha is deified as God the other being. Hinayana Buddhism in which Buddha is regarded as the religious leader or preacher. The Mahayana Buddhism was promulgated by the Saint Nagarjunacharya in the second century AD. A model of the now-submerged valley and its picturesque surroundings can also be seen in the museum.

Nagarjunasagar Srisailam Wildlife Sanctuary: This sumptuous sanctuary, home to a number of fascinating wildlife species spreads over an undulating sylvan landscape ranging between 200 and 900 meters in altitude is surrounded by Mahaboobnagar, Kurnool, Prakasam, Guntur and Nalakonda districts. A scenic lake is also to view on way to Srisailam from Nagarjunasagar.

By road Nagarjunasagar is about 22 km from Macherla, 150 km from Hyderabad and 180 km from Vijayawada. There are regular busses beween Macherla and here. The nearest railway station is at Macherla and the nearest airport is at Hyderabad.

Bhattiprolu: This is yet another ancient sacred Buddhist spot, located on the banks of river Krishna, North of Repalle Taluk, about 320 km from Hyderabad. The 'Mahastupa' here, as holds one of the ancient inscriptions, has yielded several sacred relics of the Buddha. The huge dome of the massive stupa measures to 40 m in diameter. The 2.4 m drum with oblong stone slab panelling, juxtaposed with pilasters is a captivating sight. A fascinating find of the excavation is the three stone receptacles replete with inscriptions, one of which brandished a number of awesome articles such as the blackstone casket, copper beads, precious pearls and ornate jewellery, glittering flowers made of gold, two thin pieces of gold with three pieces of bones, and other jewellery.

Mangalagiri: The Mangalagiri 13km south of Vijayawada is famous for the renowned temple Lakshmi Narasimha, one of the Nine incarnations of Vishnu. This temple built by the Reddi Chiefs in the 14th century on a hillock was remodelled in the 17th century to 18th century. The devotees believe that the deity accepts only half the quantity of 'Panaka' (jaggery dissolved in water) offered by devotees. There is a small Garuda Shrine in front resembling a chariot.

Pedapulivarru: This place is where the beautiful temple dedicated to Lord Narendreswara Swamy, who is one of the various forms of Lord Siva, is situated. The temple structure has been so ingeniously engineered that the sun's rays fall directly on 'Lingam' at sunrise every Sankranthi day. The temple also has a huge branze image of Lord Nataraja.

Undavalli: This beautiful location is on the vast banks of the wonderful river Krishna. The enthralling caves of the sumptuous sylvan region with their excellent architecture and sculpture draw a comparison with those of the world famous Ajanta caves. The Vishnukundin rulers of 420 AD are believed to have been closely involved with these magnificent caves.

Accommodation

Guntur (STD : 0863)

- **Hotel Vijayakrishna Internatio-nal (3 Star)**
  Collectorate Road,
  Guntur - 522 004.
  ☎: 2222221, 2225102
  Fax: 2356741
- **Hotel Aditya**
  3/7, Brodipet,
  Guntur-522 002.
  ☎: 2232644/2232664/
  2232648/2232675
- **Hotel Ravi Sankar**
  5/1, Brodipet,
  Guntur-522 002.
  ☎: 2231750/2226000/2226027/
  2226070/2226074
- **Hotel Sindoori**
  4/7, Brodipet,
  Guntur - 522 002.
  ☎: 2245599/2254233-36
- **Hotel Viceroy**
  5-98-50/1, Main Road,
  Guntur - 522 002.
  ☎: 2238899/2242888/
  2244444

Medak

Medak, again a district known by the name of its headquarters which is about 70 km from Hyderabad on the way to Mumbai has places of varied interests. The church popularly known as *Medak Church* situated in a scenic region whose construction took 10 long years has an interesting legend associated with it. This massive church which can hold upto 5000 people at a time has wonderful glass windows and splendid paintings illustrating events from the 'Holy Bible'.

This district cannot evade the foraging eyes of archaeologists since a number of antique articles have been unearthed at the excavation site at Kondapur. These articles take one back to 3000 BC.

The 'Bison Range' at Popikondalu is replete with picturesque regions of nature's bounty. The beautiful river Godavari courses elegantly along the valley of the mountains giving rise to serene lakes.This region offers exciting scenery to stand and admire.

Medak comes under the meteorological subdivision Telangana which experiences a pleasant climate from November to February.

In and Around Medak

Medak Cathedral : Medak had once been graced with the glorious Buddhist culture as deciphered from the archaeological excavations here. The captivating region of sylvan beauty is sanctified by the marvellous church built of exclusive white granite in the grand Gothic architectural style. According to a legend, this church with its fabulous stained glass windows was the outcome of the faithful gratitude of a large number of people who had been wailing in a seemingly unsurmountable famine which had its malicious spell for three long years during the World War - I.

The forlorn people took recourse to the Reverend Charles Walker Posnett, a British Missionary. Then, as the Almighty God, pleased by the prayers, provided them food, the Reverend proposed building the church. The proposal was spontaneously hailed and the church thus came into existence, with the conscientious hands of thankful hearts. Started in the year 1914, it was consecrated in 1924 during Christmas.

The roomy church which can hold upto 5000 people at a time has a lot of exciting features. The spiral bell tower rises to a height of 175 ft. The inspiring paintings in the church which had taken the British artist 40 years at his London Studio, recount holy events from the Bible. These pictures with a touch of sheen have been admired over the years by a number of visitors. The window in the north depicts the ascension of Lord Jesus to Heaven and it also forms a canopy to the Altar while the windows on the east and west display various events right from the birth to the crucifixion of the Lord.

Kondapur: About 90 km on the west of Hyderabad, Kondapur is the archaeological site of excavations which has yielded some antique treasures dating back to 3000 BC. Among the articles unearthed were, copper, silver and gold coins and relics of Buddhist, Roman and Satavahana Eras and also limestone sculptures and megalithic graves. Visitors come here to get lost in antiquity. Another tourist attraction here is the Kondapur museum, which is maintained by the Archaelogical Survey of India. This museum is said to contain about 8,100 antiquities at present.

Medak Fort: About 75 km from Hyderabad, this magnificent fort with five sturdy cascading walls, on a scenic hillock is said to have been built by the Kakatiyas. The hill is encircled by two of the five massive walls. Bastions can be seen at the entrance of each gateway. A flight of steps has been cut on the rocks for access in and out of the fort.

The fort also encompasses, a beautiful grand Mosque built in the 17th century, a gorgeous palace known as the Mubark-Mahal, granaries where sumptuous heaps of grains were stored and beautiful stone houses which were the residences of the olden military commanders. The gracious incline of the hill is embellished with Hindu-temple carvings. The carving of Kakatiyan emblem 'Gandabherunda', a double-headed eagle can also be seen.

Alladrug: A huge carved Nandi in front of the Veerabhadra temple is a popular tourist attraction in Alladrug. This is a place of archeological value.

Manjeera Sanctuary: A small sanctuary of river line forest on the banks of River Manjeera that homes many water bird species, mugger crocodiles and fresh water turtles.

Nizamabad

Once known as Indhrapuri or Indhur. This district is well connected by roadways, as such, bus service is one of the important methods of transportation. As this district is situated at a considerable distance from the Sea coast, the climatic condition is extreme. It rises to as high as 47 deg C during the peak summer while in the winters it is as low as 5 deg C.

Bodhan : Bodhan is a historical important site that is 32 km far from Nizamabad. It is known for housing remnants of structures, constructed by various rulers of different dynasties. The renowned Deval Masjid (mosque) is situated here. The historical sites in Bodhan include Vanda Stambala Gudi (Hundred Pillars Temple) and Shivalayam.

Vanda Stambala Gudi was built during the Kakatiya's Dynasty and is similar to the Veyyi Stambala Gudi (Thousand Pillars Temple) of Warangal. Now the temple has almost entirely disappeared.

The Shiva Lingam housed in the Shivalayam is the biggest of South India. It is said that Bodhan was once populated with a large number of devotees of Lord Shiva. As the city was flooded 7 times, the devotees of Lord Shiva established the temple on a hill.

Ali Sagar : This huge man-made reservoir with its natural surroundings offers a wonderful retreat from the hustle and bustle of city life. Built in 1930s, this reservoir is located 10 km from Nizamabad.

Archaeological and Heritage Museum: This museum houses number of artefacts representing the evolution of human civilisation right from Paleolithic to Vijaya Nagar Times.

Dichpalli Temple : A beautiful temple of Rama situated on a hillock, just off the Hyderabad-Nizamabad highway, 15 km from the town. The temple is known for its exquisite carvings on the temple walls, ceilings and door frames that are on par with Khajuraho Temple.

Sri Raghunathalayam Quilla: This 10th century fort of the Rashtrakutas reflects the Asaf Jahi style of architecture. The fort offers a panoramic view of the Nizamabad town and its surroundings. The main attraction of the fort is the Bada Rammandir Temple, built by Samarth Ramdass, the Guru of Chatrapathi Shivaji.

Mallaram Forest : Located 7 km from Nizamabad. Ensconced in Sylvan surroundings it is the perfect place for eco-tourism as well as adventure tourism.

Rock formations -Armoor Road: Popular for the water spot nearby. Local people believe that the water has curative powers, healing chronic diseases and disabilities. On top of the hillock is the Navanatha Siddeswara Temple.

Domakonda: A fort of 18th century, built by the Reddy rulers of Domakonda Samsthanam stands here. Inside the fort are two palaces and a temple complex. The temple is dedicated to Lord Shiva.

Nizamsagar: About 144 km on the north-west of Hyderabad, the resplendent reservoir, Nizamsagar formed by the magnificent dam across the ravishing river 'Manjira' which is one of the tributaries of the glorious river Godavari, makes it a sought-after picnic spot. The road across the huge dam is 14 ft in width and offers an exhilarating view of the sumptuous surroundings. Comfortable accommodation facilities are available at the site.

Vishakapatnam

This district owes its name to its headquarters Vishakapatnam which is noted for its importance ever since the historic days. The port city is known for its natural harbour. It is also the centre of a number of maritime activities. The Hindustan Shipyard, India's major shipbuilding and repair yard is situated here.

There are also ancient temples in the district located in picturesque regions. The temple at Simhachalam dedicated to Lord Narasimha was built in the 11th century. A temple dedicated to 'Lord Sathyanarayana' is situated at Annavaram. Scores of devotees undertake a special 'Vow' and perform 'Pooja' here. 'Sathyanarayana Pooja' is performed also at a number of places throughout the nation. 'Ekadasi' festivals and 'Kalyanotsavam' are very famous at Annavaram. The district has nurtured Buddhism in the past, which is overt from the grand monolithic stupas, ancient edifices and rock-cut caves at Sankara. These monuments date back to the 7th century AD. The district thus draws pilgrims to a number of parts.

Picnic makers also have a lot to relish in Vishakapatnam district. The benign Bheemunipatnam Beach which embraces the beauty of the estuary of the ravishing Gosthani river along with the ramshackle fort of 17th century giving a vivid account of ancient Dutch settlement, invites swimming hobbyists with its safe shallow waters. Even the undulating road to the beach makes the journey exciting. The 'Rishikonda Beach' with its vivacious environs attracts skiers, surfers and swimmers.

As the blue waters of Vishakapatnam are enchanting, so are the mountains and valleys. The 'Araku Valley and Borra Caves' draws comparison with the best ghat regions of the world. The gorges here combine the charms of scenic mountains and sizzling rivulets which during showers, gurgling with deluge, seem to play 'hide and seek' in between tunnels. There are also vast coffee plantations. A journey through the sumptuous sylvan region is ever to be relished with fun and frolic.

How to get there

Air : Airport is 16km from city centre. Vishakapatnam is air linked with Kolkata, Hyderabad and Chennai, which in turn is connected by Indian Airlines with Mumbai.

Rail: Vishakapatnam is well connected with all the important cities of India. Vishakapatnam junction railway station is on the main Kolkata to Chennai line.

Road: Vishakapatnam has well organised bus terminal. National Highway No.5 (Howrah to Chennai) passes through Vishakapatnam. The APSRTC has services to destinations within Andhra Pradesh and the cities in the neighbouring states of Orissa and Madhya Pradesh. Also regular city bus services connect places of interest in the city with each other.

Sea: Vishakapatnam is connected by sea to Kolkata, Chennai, Port Blair, Ganjam, and Kakinada among other places.

In and Around Vishakapatnam

Simhachalam: Simhachalam the mighty hill lies about 16 km north of Vishakapatnam. This hill, 244 m above sea level has a temple dedicated to 'Lord Narasimha', the Lion-and-Human-form of 'Lord Vishnu'. The temple rich in architecture belongs to the 11th century in construction. The stone

inscriptions hold many important historic events. The deity here is always inundated with fragrant sandalwood paste and has the appearance of a 'Sivalinga'. The 'Chandanayatra' which is a grand festival in March-April is the time to see the deity in 'Narasimha' form.

Government busses ply between here and Vishakapatnam. The nearest railway station and airport are also at Vishakapatnam, 16 km away.

Rama Krishna Beach: Rama Krishna Beach is located 5km from

the centre of Vishakapatnam. This beach occupying the largest part of the seafront, is a great spot to spend time leisurely. The R.K. Beach was jointly developed by the Municipal Corporation of Vishakapatnam (MCV) and the VUDA. The submarine museum here is one of its kind in the country. Sri Ramakrishna mission Ashram is located nearby.

Lawson's Bay Beach: Another important beach in the city, Lawsons Bay Beach has beautiful golden sands and lush green vegetation.

Bhimunipatnam Beach: About 24 km from Vishakapatnam, this fabulous beach is beautified by the enchanting estuary of the ravishing river Gosthani. The entire region of scenic beauty also has the ruins of a 17th century Dutch Fort, which evinces the place was one of the strongholds of the Dutch. An ancient Dutch cemetery can also be seen. This beach is a little different from the other beaches along the east coast in that the sharks which frequent the coastline are not seen here and the waters near shore are relatively shallow, safe for swimming.

Even the travel from Vishakapatnam to this beach would be quite enchanting as the road is undulating all along.

Rishikonda : Here is an exciting beach about just 8 km from Vishakapatnam. This beach has lovely settings and interests swimmers, water skiers, wind surfers and layman alike.

Araku Valley and Borra Caves: This fascinating valley lies about 127 km from Vishakapatnam. The undulating ghat road here rises to a height of 1168 m above sea level and climbs down flanked by mighty mountains and fabulous scenery to Araku Valley which is itself about 975 m above the sea level. This vast expanse of sylvan beauty is inhabited by tribal community.

About 90 km from Vishakapatnam this beautiful village Borra offers a sumptuous feast to the eyes. A ravishing rivulet here becomes a deluge during heavy downpour and disappears into the limestone caves only to emerge again about 100 m below in a gorgeous gorge. This game of 'Hide and Seek' played by the sumptuous Nature obsesses the mind with delight. A large congregation of the locals can be seen on the festival day of 'Sivarathri'. The journey from Borra to Araku valley is exhilarating, which is 30 km of sheer pleasure. The entire region is rich in flora and fauna and also in fertile and pasture lands. The Anantagiri slopes near here are redolent of its rich coffee plantations.

Dolphin's Nose: Dolphin's nose, the rocky promontory with a cliff rising 174m above the sea is the most prominent sight in Vizag. It also shelters the harbour, from where manganese and iron ore are shipped out. The lighthouse here has a beam visible more than 60km out to sea.

Fort: The fort, constructed in 1661 by the Dutch forms the oldest part of the city. It is separated from the Dolphin's Nose, by a small river which forms a sandbar. Here the remains of 18th century barracks, an arsenal, the Court House, a protestant church and cemetery can be seen. The cemetery has some European graves dating back to 1699. The fort was completely ruined.

Line of three hills: Vishakapatnam is framed by a line of **three hills**, each with a shrine sacred to a different religion.

Sri Venkateswara Konda: Sri Venkateswara Konda or Hill on the South, has a temple dedicated to Lord Venkateswara. It is believed to have been built by an European Captain Blackmoor, in 1866. This temple has a small steeply pyramidal entrance gopura. The port channel, the entrance of the inner harbour for ships and liners can be seen from here.

Mother Mary's Church: The central and the highest Ross Hill, named after a Monsieur Ross who built a house on it in 1864, has now been converted into a Roman Catholic Mother Mary's Church. The pathway to the church is lined with shrines of the stages of the cross. There were excellent views of the ship building yard from here.

Darga Konda: The north hill Darga Konda, has a mosque and the mausoleum of the Muslim saint, Baba Ishaq Madina, revered for his prophecies and venerated by Hindu and Muslim devotees alike.

Jungle trail: The trail developed on three acres of forest amidst thick vegetation is an ideal place for trekking.

Parks

The Indira Gandhi Zoological Park: The Indira Gandhi Zoological Park, 6km from the city centre spread over 425 acres of land, has over 400 varieties of animals. This is one of the largest Zoo Park in Andhra Pradesh. The well planned layout of the zoo has different enclosures for primates, carnivores, lesser carnivores, small mammals and birds close to their natural habitats. There is mini-train to facilitate people to watch the wild life.

Open on all the days except Mondays.

Visiting Hours : 09.00 to 17.00 hrs.

Vuda Park: Vuda or Taraka Rama Park, located on the Sun and Sea beach has boating and swimming facilities, a roller skating rink, artificial caves, beautiful long lawns, flower gardens and a children's park. The Playpen for children here has plastic balls and boxing bags. There is also a Musical Fountain.

Kailasagiri Hill Park: Kailasagiri park is situated at an altitude of 360ft. on Mount Kailash, a charming hillock on the sea front bordering a small valley within the city. The magnificent statues of Shiva- Parvathi are illuminated at night and is worth seeing. The Shanku Chakra Naama which symbolizes the image of Lord Vishnu in its pristine form, fully lighted at night is visible from most parts of the city. The park gives an enchanting view of the sea, beaches, lush green forests and the bustling city. Kailasagiri is a gliders paradise with excellent gliding facilities. Situated at an altitude of 130 mts., the gliding point provides ample opportunities to test the gliding skills of the gliders.

Kondakarla Bird Sanctuary: Kondakarla Bird Sanctuary is located in lush green surroundings 40 kms from Vishakapatnam. The sanctuary has a rich variety of bird species. The area has one of the biggest fresh water lakes in the state.

Museums

Vishaka Museum: Located on the Beach road, Vishakapatnam Municipal Corporation museum has historical treasures and artifacts of the region. The museum is housed in 150 year old architecturally impressive Dutch Bungalow. The collections include ancient armory, crockery, coins, silk costumes, jewelry, stuffed animals, portraits, shell of an unexploded bomb dropped by the Japanese during World War II, manuscripts, letters, diaries, scrap books as well as periodicals, maps etc which chronicle the lives of the early settlers.

Submarine Museum: INS Kusura, a Russian built submarine was turned to a museum on 27th Feb 2001. The Submarine was brought from the sea, to the sands of the Ramakrishna Beach and set up as a museum- one of its kind in Asia. It had been in use by the Indian Defence since its arrival in Vizag in 1970.

Anthropology Museum: The department of Anthropology in the Andhra University has its own specialised Anthropology Museum established in the year 1961.

Araku Tribal Museum: The Tribal Museum in Araku valley houses rich tribal tradition and number of artifacts and displays related to Eastern Ghat tribal culture.

Buddhist Places

Sankaram Buddhist Excavations: The village of Sankaram near Anakapalli, 38 km from Vishakapatnam is known for its 3C - 4C Buddhist constructions situated on two small hillocks. These constructions are believed to be made during Mahayana period. The hills, Bojjanakonda and Lingalakonda has a monastery, numerous rock- cut stupas and sanctuaries cut into the sides of the hill with Buddha images and Viharas (shelters) for the monks. The main stupa was first carved out of rock and then encased in bricks. The site, an archeologists delight have excavated several antiquities like the seals, inscribed tablets, pots, copper coins mostly of seventh century AD.

Bavikonda: Bavikonda is located 16 km.away from Vishakapatnam along the beach road leading to Bhimunipatnam. The hill acquired the name Bavikonda due to the existence of wells on the hill to collect rain water for drinking purpose. Excavations on the hill-top brought to light an extensive Buddhist establishment consisting of a Mahachaitya, stupas, chaityagrihas, a congregation hall, platforms, viharas, kitchen-cum-store complex, pottery, relic caskets, tiles, stuccos, iron objects, moulded bricks, coins etc.

Thotlakonda: The Thotlakonda Buddhist Complex situated on a hilltop in Mangamaripeta village is 15 kms from Vishakapatnam on the Vizag-Bheemili beach road. The complex has a number of stupas, Chaityas, Viharas, a congregation hall and a refectory belonging to the Himayana School, mostly excavated during1982-92. Excavations at Thotlakonda comprise pottery, beads, bangle pieces, tiles, stuccos, iron objects, sculptural remains, moulded bricks, inscriptions, coins, etc.

Pavuralakonda: Pavuralakonda or Narasimhaswamy Konda is located near Bhimli or Bhimunipatnam about 30 km. from Vizag. Excavations of the site believed to be dated between 3rd century. B.C. and 2nd C. A.D, revealed nearly 14-16 rock-cut troughs or cisterns used for collecting rainwater, foundations of viharas, with cells and common verandah, circular chaityagrihas, votive stupas, halls etc.

Tyda Nature camp: Tyda Nature camp is located 75 kms from Vishakapatnam on the Araku road. The nature camp has facilities for rock climbing, trekking and target shooting with bow and arrows. It is home for a variety of animals and birds. With the help of naturalists or guides in the camp, one can learn the language of the jungle viz., identification of calls, marks etc. and understanding interesting features of various flora and fauna of eastern ghats. There are log huts and tents set in tribal environment for tourists.

Accommodation

Vishakapatnam (STD : 0891)

- **Taj Residency (5 Star)**
  Beach Road,
  Vishakapatnam - 530 002.
  ☎: 2567756, Fax: 2564370
  E-mail: trghm.viz@tajhotels.com

- **The Park (5 Star)**
  Beach Road,
  Vishakapatnam - 530 023.
  ☎: 2554488,
  Fax: 2554181
  E-mail: admini.viz@park.sprintrpg.ems.vsnl.net.in

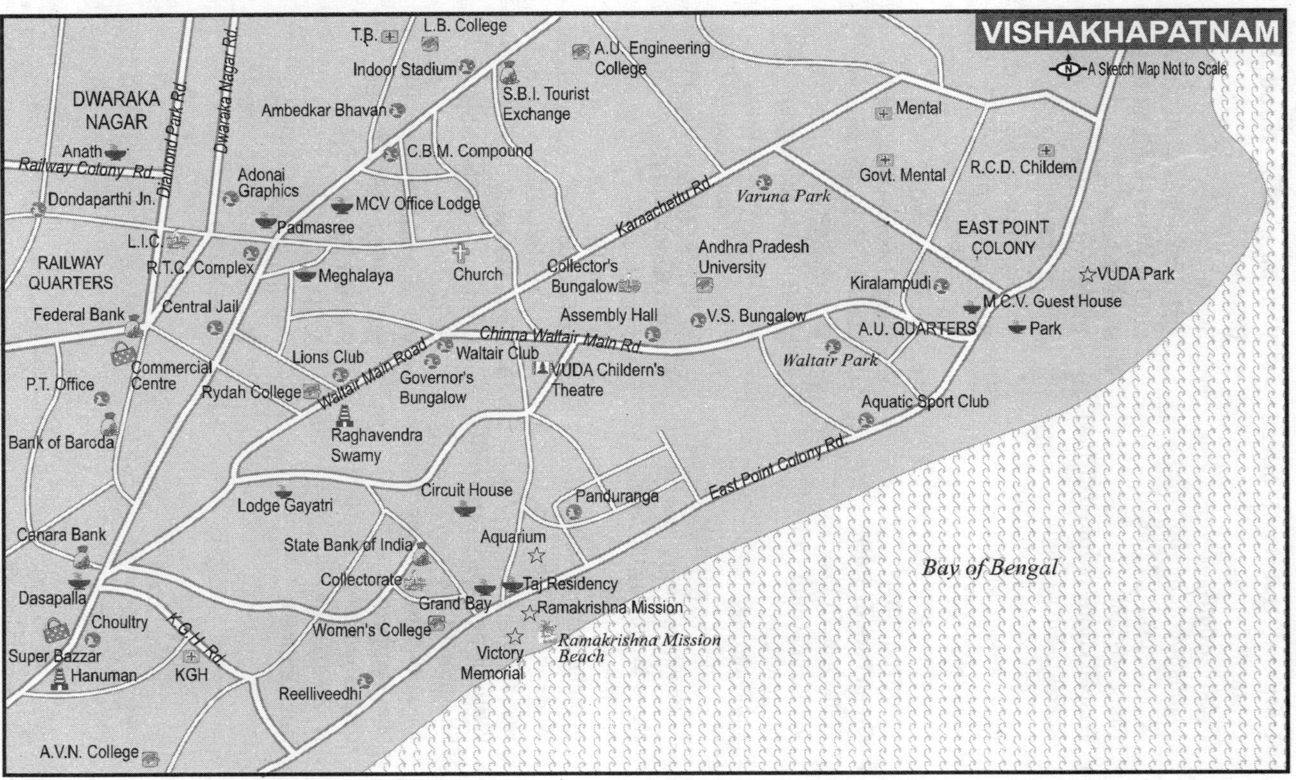
VISHAKHAPATNAM
A Sketch Map Not to Scale
T.B.
L.B. College
Indoor Stadium
A.U. Engineering College
S.B.I. Tourist Exchange
DWARAKA NAGAR
Diamond Park Rd.
Dwaraka Nagar Rd
Ambedkar Bhavan
Mental
Govt. Mental
R.C.D. Childem
Anath
Railway Colony Rd.
C.B.M. Compound
Adonai Graphics
Dondaparthi Jn.
MCV Office Lodge
Karaachettu Rd.
Varuna Park
Padmasree
EAST POINT COLONY
L.I.C.
RAILWAY QUARTERS
R.T.C. Complex
Meghalaya
Church
Collector's Bungalow
Andhra Pradesh University
VUDA Park
Kiralampudi
M.C.V. Guest House
Federal Bank
Central Jail
Assembly Hall
V.S. Bungalow
A.U. QUARTERS
Park
Chinna Waltair Main Rd
Lions Club
Waltair Club
VUDA Childern's Theatre
Waltair Park
Commercial Centre
P.T. Office
Rydah College
Waltair Main Road
Governor's Bungalow
Aquatic Sport Club
Raghavendra Swamy
Bank of Baroda
East Point Colony Rd.
Circuit House
Panduranga
Lodge Gayatri
State Bank of India
Aquarium
Canara Bank
Bay of Bengal
Collectorate
Taj Residency
Dasapalla
Grand Bay
Ramakrishna Mission
Choultry
K.G.H. Rd.
Women's College
Ramakrishna Mission Beach
Super Bazzar
Victory Memorial
Hanuman
KGH
Reelliveedhi
A.V.N. College

- **Dolphin Hotels Limited (4 Star)**
  Daba Gardens,
  Vishakapatnam - 530 020.
  ☎: 2567000 (27 lines)
  Fax: 2567555
- **Daspalla Hotels Limited (3 Star)**
  28/2/48, Surya Bagh,
  Vishakapatnam - 530 020.
  ☎: 2564825, 2563141
  Fax: 2562043
  E-mail: daspalla.vsp@rml.sprintrpg.ems.vsnl.net.in
- **Green Park (3 Star)**
  Waltair Main Road,
  Vishakapatnam - 530 002.
  ☎: 2564444
  Fax: 2563763
  E-mail: geepark.vizag@rmlsprintrpg.ems.vsnl.net.in
- **Hotel Meghalaya (3 Star)**
  Asilmetta Junction,
  Vishakapatnam - 530 003.
  ☎: 2755141-145
  Fax: 2555824
- **Welcomgroup Grand Bay Sheraton (3 Star)**
  15-1-44, Nowroji Road,
  Maharanipeta,
  Vishakapatnam - 530 002.
  ☎: 2560101,
  Fax: 2550691
- **Welcomgroup Grand Bay (3 Star)**
  Beach Road,
  Vishakapatnam - 530 023.
  ☎: 2560101 Fax: 2550691
- **Hotel Prince**
  30-12-16/17, Ranga Street,
  Daba Gardens,
  Vishakapatnam - 530 020.
  ☎: 2747675-79
  Fax: 2747674
- **Hotel Prasanth**
  Balaji Soudha-Poorna Buildings,
  Main Road, Vishakapatnam.
  ☎: 2526948
- **Hotel Jyothi Swaroopa**
  47-11-2, Dwarakanagar,
  Vishakapatnam - 530 016.
  ☎: 2748871/75 Fax: 2741040
- **Palm Beach Hotel**
  Beach Road,
  Waltair Uplands,
  Vishakapatnam - 530 001.
  ☎: 2754026/27
- **Hotel Simhagiri**
  D.No.43-9-1, Plot No.1,
  Block No.9,
  Vishakapatnam - 530016.
  ☎: 2540253/ 2505794-96
- **Sarovar Hotel**
  47-11-17,
  Vishakapatnam - 530016.
  ☎: 2551099/2755004/237/257/259/260

Vizianagaram

Vizianagaram is the district headquarters and one of the northern coastal districts of Andhra Pradesh. It is an important cultural centre, was the capital of the Rajas of Vizianagaram in the 17th century. It is located about 18 km inland from the Bay of Bengal, and 40 km northwest of Vishakapatnam. With its rich cultural heritage the Vizianagaram district has the potential to attract the eyes of the tourists.

Kumili: It is famous for having huge complex of temples, built by local devotees for a period over 10 years.

Ramatheertham: Located at 13 Km from Vizianagaram, this place is famous for the 1000 years old Sri Rama temple situated on the bavikonda hill. The beautiful koneru lake in its vicinity was constructed by the pusapati kings during 1650-1696 A.D. The unique feature of the temple is that it is built entirely upon a huge rock. Further up on the hill under a massive hanging rock one can see several Jain sculptures.

Bobbili: A fort here, 60 Km from town is associated with the historic battle between the Raja of Bobbili and Zamindar of Vizianagaram, who is aided by the French. The fierce war established this as a land of heroism, bravery and courage. The magnificent Bobbili fort stands as a silent testimony to this hard fought battle, which saw the Raja of bobbili, sacrifice his life fighting rather than surrendering. The Venugopala Swamy temple here is quite famous as also the oldest in the district.

Punyagiri: Located 25 Km from Vizianagaram. This place has been credited with one of the oldest Shiva temples. The sanctum has an underground water source which ensures that the Shivalinga is perpetually bathed with water. In the nearby Trimurthi cave, three lingas are installed over which water constantly drops. A large number of devotees visit here during the Mahasivaratri festival. Legend has it that if one bathes in the waterfall nearby and then has Darshan of Lord Shiva, he attains Moksha.

Ammavari Gudi Temple: The presiding deity of the temple is Paidi Thalli. The famous Sirimanu festival is celebrated here during which a big procession is taken out. The priest sits at the end of a long inclined wooden pole and the followers worship the deity by throwing bananas at him. The famous Puli Vesham dance is performed during the festival.

Mahbubnagar

Formerly known as Rukmammapeta and Palamooru this southern district of Hyderabad is bordered with River Krishna in the south and surrounded by the Nalgonda, Hyderabad, Kurnool, Raichur and Gulbarga districts. The Mahabubnagar region was once known as Cholawadi or the land of Cholas. It is said that the famous Kohinoor diamond and other famous diamonds came from Mahabubnagar district.

Alampur : The 'Nava Brahma' Temple located at the awesome confluence of the sacred and splendid rivers Tungabadra and Krishna where the former veers as if impatient to meet the mighty Krishna, is one of the grand structures of worship raised by the Chalukyas. The gorgeous architecture and the stupendous sculpture hold the peering eyes fixed upon them.

'Nava Brahma' also draws a different explanation that, according to the legend, these are the names of the medicinal herbs put forth by Rasa Siddhas.

This historic place on the banks of the beautiful river Tungabhadra is replete with ancient monuments particularly with those of the Chalukyan era. The temples are rich in excellent architecture and sculpture. The beautiful Sikaras of these temples are of a curvilinear form inundated with astounding architectural workmanship. The miniature pillars, niches, windows, and amlakas deserve a special mention. The layout, architecture and the stone carvings bear a close resemblance to those of the Buddhist and Brahmanical caves of Western India. APTDC offers accommodation. Mahbubnagar district is adjacent to Hyderabad.

Gadwal: A popular place for cotton and silk sarees in alluring designs. Located 60 km from Kurnool. Gadwal is famous for Chenna Kesava Swamy temple built by the Rajahs of Gadwal in the 17th century A.D.

Kollapur : The 16th century Madhava Swamy temple is situated here. The temple walls have beautiful sculptures depiciting the 24 aspects of Vishnu and the Dasa-Avatars of Vishnu.

Wanaparti: The Sarla Sagar Project the biggest siphon dam is nearby. The ancient Vittaleswara temple is in Wanaparti.

Nellore

Nellore derives its name from the extensive paddy cultivation in the district. It is an important commercial center. Nellore is 210km from Chennai and 515km from Hyderabad. Talpagiri Ranganathaswamy temple and its architecture is worth visiting.

Nelapattu Bird Sanctuary: Established in 1976, it is a small water bird sanctuary. It is located about 20 km north of Pulicat Bird Sanctuary. Grey pelicans, egrets, little cormorants, spoon-bills, storks, herons and many other birds are seen here.

Venkatagiri: The handloom industry produces sarees those are popular as Venkatagiri sarees.

Udayagiri: Udayagiri, in Nellore district which is an integral part of coastal Andhra, was formerly a fortified town. The once magnificent fort which had about 13 distinct strongholds stands now in ruins. The tantalising hill with its elegant cliffs, which at places are 305 m high, present a beautiful sight. In the 14th century this place saw the birth of a new kingdom founded by Langula Gajapathy who made it the capital. The hill is topped by an ancient Mosque whose construction, according to the Persian inscriptions inside, was in 1660.

Penchalakona : This beautiful village located 50 km from Nellore, is surrounded by mountains and eye-catching dense forests. It houses the temple of Sri Penusila Narasimha Swamy at the foot of a hill in the Penchalakona valley.

Mypad Beach: 25 km from Nellore this beautiful beach facing a verdant expanse of vegetation and golden grains of abundant sand attracts a large number of visitors. Mypad has road and rail links with Nellore. The nearest airports are at Tirupati and Chennai which are about 130 km and 200 km respectively.

Pulicat Lake: This is a saltwater lake in a beautiful bird sanctuary which spreads over an area of 461 sq. km near Tada, Nellore district. This sanctuary is the seasonal hangout of about 75 species of birds.

Accommodation

Nellore (STD : 0861)

- **Hotel Murali Krishna (3 Star)**
  Besides Leela Mahal,
  V.R.C. Centre, Nellore - 524 001.
  ☎: 2309030-37
  Fax: 2321137
- **Hotel Shivam International (P) Ltd. (3 Star)**
  18/11, Achari Street,
  Nellore - 524 001.
  ☎: 2320320 (7 Lines)
  Fax : 2348999
- **Hotel Simhapuri (3 Star)**
  Railway Station Road,
  Nellore - 524 001.
  ☎: 2327040-45

- **Uthama Hotel (3 star)**
  23/976, Dhandayudha Puram,
  Nellore - 524 003. ☎: 2317777
- **Hotel Abhiram**
  23/931, Achari Road,
  Nellore - 524 001.
  ☎: 2347477-82
- **Hotel Anurag**
  16/343, Jawharlal Road,
  Nellore - 524 001.
  ☎: 2327975/2327572-75

Cuddapah

This district is located 8 km south of the Penna River and is surrounded on three sides by the Nallamala and Palakonda hills. It is said to be the heart of the Rayalaseema as it is centrally located and well connected with the 4 districts of Rayalaseema.

This District has a glorious history and a rich cultural heritage. It is identified as a part of Dandakaranya through which the Lord Rama and his consort Sita wandered during their exile. Holy rivers like Penna (Panakini), Papaghni, Chitravati, Mandavya cut across the district giving the land sanctity of their own. Kunderu, Sagileru are the chief Northern tributaries to Penna and Cheyyeru, Papaghni and Chitravathi are the Southern tributaries . This district was a part of the Chola Empire and Kakatiya empire from the 11th to 14th century.

It is a district administrative center and a market for peanuts, cotton, and melons. Paint and varnish are manufactured, and barite is processed. Primary languages spoken in the city are Telugu and Urdu (because of its large Muslim population). English is spoken and used as a medium of education in many of its educational institutions.

One of the biggest celebrations in Kadapa is Kadapotsavalu. This is started mainly to remove the bad opinion on Kadapa that it is a faction district and to show the culture and traditions of Kadapa. It is started in the year 2003. Several thousands of people including the celebrities from all over the India take part in the celebrations that lasts for 5 days. There are various stalls on the streets of Kadapa with thousands of people there. These celebrations are focussed mainly in the media during Kadapostavalu.

Picnic makers have a lot in Kadapa. Besides a number of temples there are Wildlife Sanctuaries and places of historical importance too.

Sri Lankamalleswara Wildlife Sanctuary: Sri Lankamalleswara Wildlife Sanctuary is located 15 km from Cuddapah railway station. These dry, deciduous mixed thorn forests have panther, sloth bear, chital, sambar, chowsingha, chinkara, nilgai, wild boar and fox. This sanctuary is famous for its critically endangered Jerdon's Courser , locally known as Kalivi kodi. The sanctuary is named after the Sri Lankamalleswaraswami temple located inside it. This temple was built by Janmejayamaharaj and is located close to a waterfall.

October to March will be the ideal time to visit this sanctuary. Forest rest houses are available at Siddavatam and Cuddapah.

Pushpagiri Temple complex: Pushpagiri Temple complex is situated 16 km northwest of Cuddapah town on the banks of the Pennar River. Located on hill, this complex houses eight temples that are collectively known as Pushpagiri Temple.

This temple complex, built by the Cholas, is renowned for its detailed sculptures. The temples are those of Kasi Viswanatha, Rangaswami, Vaidhyanatha, Trikoteswara, Bhimeswara, Indranateswara, Kamalasambhaveswara, Shiva and Kesavaswami. The temples of Pushpagiri have sculptures from the episodes of the Ramayana, Mahabharata and Bhagavata. Sivaratri and Vaikunda Ekadasi are the festivals celebrated here.

Sidhot Fort: Located near Siddavatam, around 25 km from Cuddapah. This fort stands on the banks of river Pennar and covers an area of 30 acres. This fort is often referred to as the gateway to Srisailam or Dakshina Kasi. This fort encompasses beautifully sculptured temples of Siddheswara, Bala Brahma, Ranganayaka Swamy and a Durga Temple that attracts numerous pilgrims.

Gandikota Fort: Gandikota or 'The Gorge Fort' is situated about six miles to the west of Jammalamadugu in Cuddapah district. The width within the fort is at its broadest, about five and a half furlongs from west to east and almost a mile from northwest to southeast.The area within is full of the debris of ages and many ancient structures in varying stages of decay. The fort has a Masjid, a large granary and a temple. The Jamia Masjid has two adjacent minarets. Within the fort are two ancient temples, dedicated to Madhava and Raghunatha. This fort also houses the structures of a magazine, a graceful 'pigeon tower' with fretted windows and an extensive palace built by bricks with some plastered decorations and some wells. There is an old cannon still lying in the fort. There is also the 'Rayalacheruvu' with its perennial springs irrigating some lime and plantain gardens.

Nandalur Temple: About 42 km from the District headquarters of the Cuddapah district is this famous temple of Sri Soumyanatha Swamy. This temple built by the Matli kings is the main attraction of the village. The Presiding deity here is Sri Soumyanatha Swamy and Sri Maha Lakshmi Ammavaru.

The temple is old and holds quite a bit of archealogical importance.

Tallapaka Temple: Located 3 km from Cuddapah town Tallapaka village has the distinction of being the birthplace of Saint Annamacharya, the famous composer of devotional songs on Lord Venkateswara during the 15th century.

The Siddheswaraswamy temple with Lord Shiva as its presiding deity is one among the famous temples in Tallapaka. The side wall of the temple has a hole through which sun rays enter during the month of Karthik, a holy time in November when married women pray for the long life of their husbands and give offerings to the Lord.

Nalgonda

Yadagirigutta: Nalgonda district, about 70 km from Hyderabad, like Medak, falls in the Telengana region in the meteorological classification, where pleasant climate can be experienced between November and February while April and May, the peak of summer, are scorching. Humidity is high from July to September.

Yadagirigutta, the famous pilgrim centre is beautifully nestled among numerous blue hills. The temple here is dedicated to 'Lord Lakshminarayana', a variation of Lord Vishnu.

Legend has it that Gandaberunda, Yogananda and Jwala, three of the nine aspects of Lord Vishnu are manifested here. An oil lamp burns eternally to mark the manifestation of Jwala or Light. It is also believed that worshipping the Lord at this shrine is the panacea to cure all malicious diseases.

Kolanupaka: It is an important pilgrim center and has a well maintained Jain temple and many Hindu temples.

Nagarjunasagar Dam: This dam built across the Krishna River is 124m high and the tallest masonry dam in the world.

Ethipothala Waterfalls: About 6 km northwest of Macherla this

gorgeous waterfalls is created by the mighty river Krishna and the sizzling rivulet Chandravanka which has its captivating confluence with Krishna at a point before the ravishing falls where the turbulent waters fall from a height of 21 metres.

Nandikonda: Situated 8.5km from Nagarjunasagar, these are the remains of the Ikshvaku citadel and many Buddhist monasteries and halls.

Pillalamarri: Pillalamari is famous for the 5000 years old Banyan tree which covers an area of over 3 acres. The tree can accommodate about 1000 people under its shade.

Rachakonda: Another location depicting the Kakatiya art and architecture. The 'Dasavathara' sculptures in a cave and the five temples in the town are of touristic interest.

Prakasam

This district was named after the great patriot Tanguturi Prakasam Panthulu, also known as Andhra Kesari. Ongole, the headquarters of this district is located 138 km from Vijayawada. Ongole is an ancient town which finds mention in the inscriptions of the Pallava rulers of the 3rd and 4th century A.D.

Chandavaram: Located in Prakasam district, Chandavaram, about 90 km from Ongole is also one of the historic places where ancient Buddhist monuments can be seen. This beautiful place is also an excavation site where over 30 exquisitely carved limestone panels were unearthed. These panels were once the ornate decorations over the dome of a 'Stupa'. The unique stupa on a picturesque hillock known as the 'Sinkarakonda' which literally means 'beautiful hill' overlooking the ravishing rivulet 'Gundlakaa' has two terraces and draws comparison with the famous Dhararajaka Stupa at Taxila. There are also several other smaller stupas and a Monastery complex in the proximity.

Government buses ply between here and Vijayawada where accommodations are available.

Motupalle: Located 45 km from Ongole, Motupalle is an ancient seaport that flourished under various dynasties from 1st century AD. Buddhist ruins indicate that it was a Buddhist center in the old days.

Accommodation

- **Sri Venkateswara Hotel**
  Ongole Road, Giddalur,
  Prakasam - 523 394.
  ☎: 242100
- **Sid & Dip Beach Resort**
  Vodarevu, Prakasam - 523 394.
  ☎: 248222
- **Hotel Maurya**
  Opp. RTC Bus Stand,
  Ongole. ☎: 2233535
- **Hotel Purnima**
  Near RTC Bus Stand
  Ongole. ☎: 2233666

Srikakulam

Srikakulam district came into being in 1950. Until then it was part of Vishakapatnam. Srikakulam town is the district headquarters. The nearest airport is Vishakapatnam at 106km. Roads and rail connect the city to other parts of the state.

Srikakulam is a place where gushing rivers meet dense wooded hills, where the golden sands of the beaches are coupled with a variety of flora and fauna.

Arasaville: The ancient Sun-God temple is famous and attracts many devotees from all over the country.

Srikurmam: A pilgrim center for devotees of Lord Vishnu. The inscriptions on the temple shed light on the various kingdoms those ruled the region.

Srimukhalingam: The 9th century Srimukhalingeswara temple of Indo-Aryan style has remarkable sculptures.

Srikurmanandha Swamy Temple: This magnificent temple of Lord Vishnu is an important pilgrim centre of Srikakulam. It is famous for its architectural beauty and the peace of mind it provides. It, contains over 200 pillars and many inscriptions in Devanagri script dating from the iith to the 19th century A.D. It lies 15 km away from Srikakulam. It has a huge five storey Gopuram built in typical South Indian style of architecture. The wall paintings resemble those at the Ajanta Caves. A popular legend has it that if bones of the deceased are thrown in Swetapushkarani tank, they get converted into Kurmas or Tortoises.

Telineelapuram & Telukunchi: Telineelapuram & Telukunchi are well known bird sanctuaries. Telineelapuram is located 65 km from Srikakulam. Telukunchi is at a distance of 115 km from Srikakulam. As there are a number of fish ponds in Telineelapuram & Telukunchi areas, Pelicans and Painted Storks migrate every winter season from Siberia to nest and breed. Naturally, these sanctuaries are a favourite of avid bird watchers.

Mahendra Hills: Located about 90 km from Srikakulam town, this hills is regarded as the highest peak in the Eastern Ghats. This scenic hill is an excellent spot for bird watching. It is believed that the Pandavas during their exile stayed here. A temple dedicated to Lord Shiva is set in pristine natural surroundings on the hilltop. The rock formations and Buddhist meditation center here are the other attractions.

Salihundam: Located 18 km from Srikakulam on the banks of the river Vamsadhara, this village shot into prominence because excavations revealed the existence of an ancient Bhuddhist settlement. Significantly, this was the place from where the message of Bhuddhism spread to Sumatra and other eastern countries.

Budithi: This is a tiny village located 42 km from from Srikakulam where the inhabitants life revolves around creating beautiful vessels out of alloys. The shapes being created here ranges from the charmingly traditional to the elegantly modern. Usually made of brass, the objects have unique patterns forming simple and striking presentations. Floral patterns made here needs a special mention.

Adilabad

Adilabad district is the northern tip of Andhra Pradesh. It is connected by NH7 to Hyderabad. Other places of the state are also connected with Adilabad by road.

Basar: The temple here is one of the two famous ones dedicated to Goddess Saraswathi, the Goddess for 'Arts and Learning' and the consort of Lord Brahma, the creator of the Universe. The other Saraswathi Temple can be seen in Kashmir.

The legend has it that the Sage Vyasa used to collect three handfuls of the river sand after his usual bath in the sacred river Godavari as part of his everyday routine. The sand thus accumulated turned into the images of Goddess Saraswathi, Goddess Lakshmi and Goddess Kali. 'Brahmapuranam' puts forth that 'Adikavi Valmiki' installed the presiding deity here and it was here, he wrote the great epic 'The Ramayana'.

The image of the Sage Valmiki and his 'Samadhi' can be seen near the temple which according to a belief is one of the three temples built by the Rashtrakutas near the confluence of the sacred rivers Manjira and Godavari. Contrary to this, another belief exists, by which this temple had been built by a Karnataka King by name 'Bijialudu' who ruled the province of Nandagiri with Nanded as his capital. In the Sanctum Sanctorum, the image of Goddess Lakshmi can be seen besides Goddess Saraswathi.

Since this place is graced by Goddess Saraswathi, the Goddess for Arts and Learning, Goddess Lakshmi, the Goddess for Wealth and Goddess Kali, the Goddess for Bravery, Basar is revered as the Holy abode of divine Trinity where the devotees are blessed with all the three vital traits.

The temple festival during February-March and September-October attracts large crowds of pilgrims from all over the country.

Kunthala Waterfalls: This is the highest waterfall in Andhra Pradesh. It drops from a height of 45 meters and is near Kunthala village on the banks of Kadam river.

Nirmal: Nirmal town is known for its fort built by the French engineers in the Nisam's service. Nirmal is also famous for toys and Nirmal Plates(plates with miniature paintings and floral design) which flourished with the availability of light wood in the area.

Kawal Sanctuary: The sanctuary, established in 1965, is 260 km from Hyderabad and is accessible by road. It spreads over 893sq.km with dry deciduous teak forest, bamboo and miscellaneous species of flora. Cheetah, sambar, nilgai, muntjac(barking deer), Indian bison(Gaur), sloth bear, panther, tiger and variety of birds are seen in the sanctuary.

Pranahitha Sanctuary: Another wildlife sanctuary situated approximately 300 km from Hyderabad. The habitat is dry deciduous teak forests spread over 136sq. km along the Pranahita River with undulating terrain. Cheetah, black buck, nilgai, sloth bear, panther, tiger and birds including brahmin ducks, teals, storks and herons are seen here.

Sivaram Wildlife Sanctuary: Located along the River Godavari, this Wildlife Sanctuary is spread approximately 36.29 square kilometers, noted for Marsh Crocodiles, available throughout Indo-Gangetic plain.

The fresh water crocodile also known as Mugger Crocodile, can crawl for considerable distances on land. Being equally mobile on land and water, these crocodiles are a hot tourist attraction. Besides, there are wide collection of fauna consists of Panther, Sloth bear, Nilgai, Cheetal, Rhesus Monkey etc. The preferable time for a visit to this Wildlife Sanctuary is from December to April.

Karimnagar

Karimnagar has the biggest thermal power station in Andhra Pradesh. The city is linked by road to other parts of the state.

Karimnagar town is said to have been founded by Syed Karimuddin, a Qiladar and is situated at a distance of 160 km from Hyderabad. It was formerly known as "Sabbinadu". Inscriptions of the Kakatiya king Prola II and Prataparudra found at Karimnagar and Srisailam respectively testify this fact. The city is an agricultural center and the surrounding region is mainly agricultural area on the Deccan Plateau, and is drained by the Godavari River.

Dharmapuri: Situated in the western bank (Right Bank) of the sacred river Godavari, Dharmapuri is one of the oldest villages in Andhra Pradesh, located about 29 km from Jagtial town. It is one of the places in South India where Khumb Mela takes place. It has a very ancient Sri Lakshmi Nrusimha temple, ancient Sri Sitarama temple are very famous one in the District of Karimnagar.

Elgandal: A fort on a hill, Brindaban Tank are some of the historical remains that can be seen here. The fort is situated on the banks of the Manair river amidst palm groves at a distance of 10 km from Karimnagar on the KamaReddy road. This place is historically important because 5 important dynasties ruled over this place.. Besides, there are temples of Nelakantha Swamy and Narasimha Swamy.

Dhulikatta: This holy Buddhist location is located 20 km from Karim-nagar. The three day Satavahana festival is held here every year in January. Being an important Buddhist site, Dhulikatta contains many Buddhist stupas of the Satavahana period and one of the 30 walled cities mentioned by Megasthanes in his travel account, the Indica. Excavations have dated the site to have flourished between the 2nd Century BC to 2nd Century AD.

Elgandal Fort

Khammam

Khammam is an ancient town that was an important administrative center during the reign of Kakatiyas in the 13th century. Khammam is 257km from Hyderabad by rail. Roads link the city to other parts of the state.

Kinnerasani Sanctuary: A wildlife sanctuary of 655sq.km, situated near Paloncha in Khammam district. The sanctuary includes thc big reservoir kinnersani. Many animals including tigers and leopards live here.

Bhadrachalam: Situated about 161 km from Rajahmundry and 300 km from Hyderabad, this holy

place has many prehistoric and historic references. The famous ancient temple here dedicated to Sri Seetha Ramachandraswamy is situated on the beautiful banks of the wonderful river Godavari. This popular pilgrim spot is where an estimated three lakh devotees congregate to witness the holy 'Kalyana Mahotsava,' a grand annual festival which is indeed the marriage anniversary of Lord Rama and His consort Goddess Sita. It is believed that Bhadrachalam was the venue of the divine marriage in the 'Puranic era'.

The legend recounts, Lord Rama manifested here long after He had shed mortal coils, to save a devotee by name 'Badhra Maharishi' and conferred upon him the 'Eternal Bliss', the 'Moksha' and the place came to be known after the Maharishi, as Bhadrachalam. There is also an allusion that Lord Rama once appeared in the dream of a woman called 'Pokala Damakka' and enlightened her of the existence of the idols of the present temple on the Bhadragiri hills. Taken by a pleasant surprise on witnessing the idols of the deity on the exact spot as she saw in her dream, she raised a modest structure. This was the origin of this temple.

Later, during the rule of Abdul Hassan Tanashah, in the 17th century, the tahsildar renovated the temple in a grand manner. But as the tahsildar, by name Gopanna, more popular as Ramdas used the revenue money of 6 lakh rupees for the renovation, he was arrested and put behind bars. After about 12 years, Lord Rama appeared in the dream of the king and produced a receipt denoting the due amount in the form of gold coins known as '*Ramamada*'. The next morning the Sultan personally rushed to the cell to which Ramdas was confined and set him free. Astonished as he was, the Sultan presented to

Ramdas a number of gifts and also his position again as the tahsildar. Stopping not there, the Sultan also declared several grants to the temple which carried on even under the Nizam rule. Some of the jewels presented to the deities here by the ardent devotee Ramdas, which include Kalikiturai Pachala Pathakam, Chintaku Pathakam can be seen in the temple even today.

The temple is situated on a hill top surrounded by 24 smaller shrines. The tranquil temple and its splendid environs make sublime impressions. 48 forms of idols of Lord Vishnu can be seen here. 'Sri Rama Navami', the birth anniversary of Lord Rama and 'Kalyana Mahotsavam' the wedding anniversary of Lord Rama with Goddess Sita are two main festivals here.

Khammam Fort: The fort here was built in 950 A.D. by the Kakatiyas has a long and checkered history. The fort is situated on the hill known as Stambhadri. The tall, pillar-like stones found on this hill were used as pillars to support the ceiling of the temples and mandapas here. There are a few temples in the fort. Khammam town is about 257 km east of Hyderabad.

Parnasala: Located 36 km from Bhadrachalam, Parnasala is a small village, accessible by road as well as by boat. Legend has it that Lord Rama spent his 14 years of exile at Parnasala. It is believed that this was the place where Rama killed Mareecha, who came disguised as golden deer to lure Sita. A sparkling stream, passing through dense forests, presents a beautiful sight.

Kushumanchi: Just 20 km from Khammam is Kushumanchi, where one of the biggest Sivalingam is installed in the temple that was built during the Kakatiya period.

Nilakandapalle: The tourism importance of this place is its archaeological glimpses known as Virataraju dibba and Keechaka Gundam claiming importance in the days of Mahabharatha. It is located 21 km from Khammam.

The old Relics unearthed at these places strengthen the belief that this place was noted as far back the days of Mahabharata. Some Buddhist Stupas and idols found in the excavations in 1977 had further supported the belief that this district had mythological and historical past. Nelakondapalli is also famous of being the birthplace of Kancharla Gopanna, popularly known as Bhakta Ramadas. The old Residence of Bhakta Ramadas was named as Bhakta Ramadas Dhyana Mandir.

Perantalapally Papi Hills: A remote tribal village, situated 80 km from Bhadrachalam. There is some historical background behind the formation of this remote village. Perantalapally is endowed with plenty of natural wealth and resources with delightful scenaries. Keeping in view, the importance of the place, the District Tourist Department has recently started a package tour from Bhandrachalam to Papi hills through Perantalapally.

The region of this place was under darkness eight decades ago covered by dense forest. During the year 1927, the Saint Sri Swamy Balananda Yogi visited this place and strived hard for its development and for ameliorating the living standards of tribals here.

The divine atmosphere prevalent at the Ashram here immenses the visitors in an expressible joy and gives a pleasant experience. The history reveals the fact that Bhakta Sabari had been turned as river and mixed in Gowtami nearby. At about 3 km away from the place, two mountains named after Vali and Sugreeva will appear. Legends has it that at the time of searching for Sita, Lord Rama Killed Vali and entrusted the kingdom to Sugreeva and the mountains have remained as the symbols of the ancient episode.

During the journey from Kunavaram to Kolluru, the width of Godavari in between the two banks will be less than one km thereby getting narrowed up to the nearest minimum at Papi hills. A kind of pleasant experience that journey goes on in a brisky way in between the two towers will be enjoyed at the spot.

During the return journey, one can have the darshan of Lord Yoga Rama at the pilgrimage centre Sri Rama giri. People believe that Lord Rama used to be under Yoga Samadhi while he was spending the days in Dandakaranya.

The bird 'Jathyuvu' was stated to have fought against Ravana nearer to Sri Ramagiri and fell tired getting its wings broken, while Sita was being taken away. Hence this place was used to be termed as Sokkanapalli at first and later as Rekhapalli.

Train Timings

The days of operations given within brackets below the Train Nos. are with regard to the **ORIGINATING** stations whereas the Arrival and Departure correspond to the **RESPECTIVE** stations.

All the trains are express trains unless otherwise mentioned.

Abbreviations

1) Ahm - Ahmadabad	30) Hyd - Hyderabad
2) Alp - Alappuzha	31) Idr - Indoor
3) Bbn - Bhubaneswar	32) Jdp - Jodhpur
4) Bjp - Bijapur	33) Jmt - Jammu Tawi
5) Bkr - Bokaro Steel City	34) Jpr - Jaipur
6) Blp - Bilaspur	35) Kch - Kacheguda
7) Blr - Bangalore	36) Kgz - Kagaznagar
8) Bnr - Bikaner	37) Kkd - Kakinada
9) Brn - Barauni	38) Klp - Kolhapur
10) Cbe - Coimbatore	39) Knk - Kanniyakumari
11) Cgh - Chandigarh	40) Kon - Konark
12) Chn - Chennai	41) Krn - Kurnool
13) Ctr - Chitoor	42) Lkn - Lucknow
14) Dbd - Dhanbad	43) LmT - Lokmanya Tilak
15) Ddn - Dehradun	44) Lnd - Londa
16) Ddr - Dadar	45) Mch - Machilipatnam
17) Del - Delhi	46) Mdk - Mudkhed
18) Dgh - Dibrugarh	47) Mdr - Madurai
19) Dmb - Dharmabad	48) Mmb - Mumbai
20) Dud - Dudhani	49) Mng - Mangalore
21) Enk - Ernakulam	50) Mnm - Manmad
22) Gkl - Guntakal	51) Mys - Mysore
23) Gkp - Gorakhpur	52) Mzp - Muzaffarpur
24) Gnt - Guntur	53) Nad - Nandad
25) Gwt - Guwahati	54) Ngc - Nagercoil
26) Hbl - Hubli	55) Nrs - Narsapur
27) HNm - H.Nizamuddin	56) Nzd - Nizamabad
28) Hta - Hatia	57) Oka - Okha
29) Hwr - Howrah	58) Pdy - Puducherry

Abbreviations

59) Pkl	- Pakala	68) Tnl	- Tenali
60) Pls	- Palsa	69) Tpt	- Tirupathi
61) PNm	- Prasanti Nilayalam	70) Trc	- Tiruchirappalli
62) Pri	- Puri	71) Tvm	- Thiruvananthapuram
63) Ptn	- Patna	72) Var	- Varanasi
64) Rjk	- Rajkot	73) Vas	- Vasco-da-Gama
65) RNT	- Rajendra Nagar Terminus	74) Vjd	- Vijayawada
66) Sec	- Secunderabad	75) Vsk	- Visakhapatnam
67) Slm	- Shalimar	76) Ypr	- Yesvantpur
B.H.	- Brief Halt	Ex	- Except

Hyderabad

Train No.	Train Name	Arr.	Dep.
2604 (Daily)	Hyd - Chn		16.55
2701 (Daily)	Mmb - Hyd	12.10	-
2702 (Daily)	Hyd - Mmb	-	14.45
2721 (Daily)	Hyd - Hnm (Nizammudin)	-	22.30
2722 (Daily)	Hnm - Hyd	05.00	-
2723 (Daily)	Hyd - Del (A.P.)	-	06.25
2724 (Daily)	Del - Hyd (A.P.)	19.50	-
2727 (Daily)	Vsk - Hyd	06.15	-
2728 (Daily)	Hyd - Vsk	-	17.15
2759 (Daily)	Chn - Hyd (Charminar)	08.00	-
2760 (Daily)	Hyd - Chn (Charminar)	-	18.30
7031 (Daily)	Mmb - Hyd	05.55	-
7032 (Daily)	Hyd - Mmb	-	20.40
7229 (Daily)	Enk - Hyd (Sabari)	13.40	-
7230 (Daily)	Hyd - Enk (Sabari)	-	12.00
7255 (Daily)	Nrs - Hyd	05.25	-
7256 (Daily)	Hyd - Nrs	-	21.45
7429 (Daily)	Hyd - Tpt (Rayalaseema)	-	17.25
7430 (Daily)	Tpt - Hyd (Rayalaseema)	10.30	-
8645 (Daily)	Hwr - Hyd	18.30	-
8646 (Daily)	Hyd - Hwr	-	10.00

Secunderabad

Train No.	Train Name	Arr.	Dep.
1019 (Daily)	Mmb - Bbn (Konark)	07.50	08.05
1020 (Daily)	Bbn - Mmb (Konark)	11.35	11.45
1405 (Th, Su)	Mmd - Kkd	09.20	09.30
1406 (W, Sa)	Kkd - Mmd	16.25	16.40
2429 (M,W,Th,Su)	Blr - HNm (Rajdhani)	07.35	07.50
2430 (Tu,W,Sa,Su)	HNm - Blr (Rajdhani)	18.35	18.50
2437 (W)	Sec - HNm (Rajdhani Exp.)	-	07.50
2438 (Su)	HNm - Sec (Rajdhani Exp.)	18.35	-
2591 (Sa)	Gkp - Blr	15.30	15.40
2592 (M)	Blr - Gkp	07.00	07.20
2647 (M)	Cbe - HNm (Kongu Exp.)	12.00	12.20
2648 (W)	HNm - Cbe (Kongu Exp.)	12.05	12.25
2703 (Daily)	Hwr - Sec (Falaknuma)	09.35	-
2704 (Daily)	Sec - Hwr (Falaknuma)	-	16.00
2705 (Daily)	Vjd - Sec	21.50	-
2706 (Daily)	Sec - Vjd	-	07.40
2707 (M,W,F)	Tpt - HNm (AP Sampark Kranti Exp)	17.25	17.55
2708 (Su,W,F)	HNm - Tpt (AP Sampark Kranti Exp)	09.15	09.30
2713 (Daily)	Vjd - Sec (Satavahana)	11.45	-
2714 (Daily)	Sec - Vjd (Satavahana)	-	16.15
2723 (Daily)	Hyd - Del (A.P.)	06.45	06.50
2724 (Daily)	Del - Hyd (A.P.)	19.15	19.20
2737 (Daily)	Kkd - Sec	06.35	-
2738 (Daily)	Sec - Kkd	-	21.15
2747 (Daily)	Gnt - Sec (Palnad)	10.35	10.45
2748 (Daily)	Sec - Gnt (Palnad)	15.05	15.15
2759 (Daily)	Chn - Hyd (Charminar)	07.15	07.20
2760 (Daily)	Hyd - Chn (Charminar)	18.50	18.55
2763 (Su,M,T,Th,S)	Tpt - Sec (Padmavathi Exp)	05.50	-
2764 (Ex-M,W)	Sec - Tpt	-	18.30
7015 (Daily)	Bbn - Sec (Visakha)	07.30	-
7016 (Daily)	Sec - Bbn (Visakha)	-	17.00
7017 (Tu,Th,F)	Rjk - Sec	10.30	-
7018 (M,Tu,Sa)	Sec - Rjk	-	14.50
7035 (Daily)	Sec - Kgz (Telangana)	-	08.20
7036 (Daily)	Kgz - Sec (Telangana)	20.20	-
7037 (Tu)	Sec - Bnr	-	23.15
7038 (Sa)	Bnr - Sec	08.50	-

Train No.	Train Name	Arr.	Dep.
7049 (Daily)	Mch - Sec	04.45	-
7050 (Daily)	Sec - Mch	-	22.45
7091 (M, W)	Sec - RNT	-	22.00
7092 (Th,Sa)	RNT - Sec	02.30	-
7201 (Daily)	Gnt - Sec (Golconda)	13.45	-
7202 (Daily)	Sec - Gnt (Golconda)	-	13.05
7203 (W)	LmT - Vjd	10.20	10.30
7204 (S)	Vjd - LmT	14.35	14.50
7205 (T)	Mmd - Kkd	09.20	09.30
7206 (M)	Kkd - Mmd	16.25	16.40
7207 (W)	Mmd - Vjd	09.20	09.30
7208 (Tu)	Vjd - Mmd	16.25	16.40
7229 (Daily)	Enk - Hyd (Sabari)	13.00	13.05
7230 (Daily)	Hyd - Enk (Sabari)	12.20	12.30
7233 (Daily)	Sec - Kgz (Bhagyanagari)	-	15.00
7234 (Daily)	Kgz - Sec (Bhagyanagari)	10.20	-
7255 (Daily)	Nrs - Hyd	05.15	05.25
7256 (Daily)	Hyd - Nrs	22.05	22.15
7405 (Daily)	Tpt - Hyd	20.40	21.00
7406 (Daily)	Hyd - Tpt	05.40	06.05

Train No.	Train Name	Arr.	Dep.
7607 (Daily)	Sec - Krn (Tungabhadra)	-	07.40
7608 (Daily)	Krn - Sec (Tungabhadra)	19.55	-
8645 (Daily)	Hwr - Hyd	18.00	18.05
8646 (Daily)	Hyd - Hwr	10.20	10.25
2513 (Su)	Sec - Gwt	-	07.30
2514 (Th)	Gwt - Sec	04.20	-
2604 (Daily)	Hyd - Chn	17.15	17.20
2603 (Daily)	Chn - Hyd	05.15	05.20
2590 (F)	Sec - Gkp	-	07.20
2589 (W)	Gkp - Sec	15.30	-
2734 (Daily)	Sec - Tpt (Narayanadri)	-	18.05
2733 (Daily)	Tpt - Sec	06.25	-
2806 (Daily)	Sec - Vsk (Janmabhoomi)	-	07.10
2805 (Daily)	Vsk - Sec	18.25	-
2735 (Tu,Th,Su)	Sec - Ypr	-	19.15
2736 (M, W, F)	Ypr - Sec	08.35	-
5015 (M)	Gkp - Ypr	17.50	18.00
5016 (Th)	Ypr - Gkp	23.15	23.25
8510 (Th, Su)	Nzd - Vsk	21.25	21.45
8509 (W, Sa)	Vsk - Nzd	08.20	08.40

Tirupati

Train No.	Train Name	Arr.	Dep.
2763 (Sa,Su,M,W,F)	Tpt - Sec (Padmavathi)	-	17.05
2764 (Tu,Th,F,Sa,Su)	Sec - Tpt (Padmavathi)	07.25	-
6053 (Daily)	Chn - Tpt	17.00	-
6054 (Daily)	Tpt - Chn	-	10.05
6057 (Daily)	Chn - Tpt (Sapthagiri)	09.30	-
6058 (Daily)	Tpt - Chn (Sapthagiri)	-	17.20
6203 (Daily)	Chn - Tpt (Intercity)	20.05	-
6351 (W, Su)	Tpt - Ngc	10.45	12.30
6352 (Th, Su)	Ngc - Tpt	21.40	22.00
6359 (Su)	Enk - Ptn	12.10	12.40
6360 (W)	Ptn - Enk	09.50	10.00
7209 (Daily)	Blr - Kkd (Sheshadri)	19.55	20.00
7210 (Daily)	Kkd - Blr (Sheshadri)	05.25	05.30
7405 (Daily)	Tpt - Hyd (Krishna)	-	05.25
7406 (Daily)	Hyd - Tpt (Krishna)	21.25	-
7429 (Daily)	Hyd - Tpt (Rayalaseema)	08.45	-
7430 (Daily)	Tpt - Hyd (Rayalaseema)	-	19.15
7479 (Ex.Tu,Th)	Hwr - Tpt	16.05	-
7480 (Ex.Th,Su)	Tpt - Hwr	-	10.35
7482 (Th,Su)	Tpt - Blp	-	10.35
7481 (Tu,Sa)	Blp - Tpt	16.05	-
7487 (Daily)	Tpt - Vsk (Thirumala)	-	20.50
7488 (Daily)	Vsk - Tpt (Thirumala)	05.00	-
2797 (Daily)	Kch - Ctr (Venkatadri)	07.30	07.35
7229 (Daily)	Tvm - Hyd (Sabari Exp.)	00.30	00.35
7230 (Daily)	Hyd - Tvm (Sabari Exp.)	00.30	00.35
6381 (Daily)	Mmb - Knk	14.30	14.35
6382 (Daily)	Knk - Mmb	03.20	03.25
2835 (Tu,Su)	Hta - Ypr	22.00	22.05
2836 (W,F)	Ypr - Hta	14.35	14.40
6688 (Th)	Jmt - Mng (Navyug)	01.20	01.22
6687 (M)	Mng - Jmt	09.08	09.10
6318 (M)	Jmt - Knk	01.20	01.22
6317 (F)	Knk - Jmt	09.08	09.10
2845 (Su)	Bbn - Ypr	03.45	03.47
2846 (Tu)	Ypr - Bbn	14.35	14.40
2660 (W)	Slm - Ngc (Gurudev)	03.45	03.47
2659 (Su)	Ngc - Slm	09.08	09.10
2646 (Tu)	Hnm - Enk	17.10	17.12

Train No.	Train Name	Arr.	Dep.	Train No.	Train Name	Arr.	Dep.
2645 (Sa)	Enk - Hnm	07.30	07.35	2836 (W,F)	Ypr - Hta	14.35	14.40
2626 (Daily)	Del - Tvm	21.05	21.07	2835 (Tu,Su)	Hta - Ypr	22.00	22.05
2625 (Daily)	Tvm - Del	03.50	03.52	2798 (Daily)	Ctr - Kch (Venkatadri)	18.30	18.35
2644 (F)	Hnm - Tvm Swarna Jayanthi	17.10	17.12	2797 (Daily)	Kch - Ctr	07.30	07.35
2643 (Tu)	Tvm - Hnm	07.30	07.35	6381 (Daily)	Mmb - Knk	14.30	14.35
2707 (M,W,F)	Tpt - Hnm	-	05.45	6382 (Daily)	Knk - Mmb	03.20	03.25
2708 (W,F,Su)	Hnm - Tpt	21.35	-	7401 (Daily)	Tpt - Mch	-	19.40
2864 (Daily)	Ypr - Hwr	02.30	02.35	7402 (Daily)	Mch - Tpt	04.35	-
2863 (Daily)	Hwr - Ypr	23.40	23.45	6734 (Sa)	Mnm - Mdu	22.00	22.05
				6733 (Th)	Mdu - Mnm	11.10	11.15

Guntakal

Train No.	Train Name	Arr.	Dep.	Train No.	Train Name	Arr.	Dep.
1013 (Daily)	LmT - Cbe	13.50	13.55	6331 (M)	Mmb - Tvm	03.50	03.55
1014 (Daily)	Cbe - LmT	21.35	21.40	6332 (Sa)	Tvm - Mmb	03.45	03.50
1043 (F)	LmT - Mdu	15.50	15.55	6339 (W,Th,F,Su)	Mmb - Ngc	03.50	03.55
1044 (Sa)	Mdu - LmT	13.15	13.25	6340 (M,Tu,W,F)	Ngc - Mmb	04.00	04.10
2591 (Sa)	Gkp - Blr	22.55	23.00	6501 (Tu)	Ahm - Blr	21.20	21.25
2592 (M)	Blr - Gkp	22.25	22.30	6502 (Su)	Blr - Ahm	19.15	19.25
2627 (Daily)	Blr - Del (Karnataka)	00.50	00.55	6513 (Su,W,F)	Ypr - Bjp (Bagava Exp.)	22.55	23.00
2628 (Daily)	Del - Blr	06.40	06.45	6514 (M,Th,Sa)	Bjp - Ypr (Bagava Exp.)	03.00	03.05

Train No.	Train Name	Arr.	Dep.
6529 (Daily)	Mmb - Blr (Udyan)	23.25	23.30
6530 (Daily)	Blr - Mmb (Udyan)	03.00	03.05
6531 (M)	Ajr - Ypr	23.00	23.05
6532 (F)	Ypr - Ajr	22.45	22.55
6591 (Daily)	Hbl - Blr (Hampi Exp.)	22.25	22.50
6592 (Daily)	Bdr - Hbl (Hampi Exp.)	04.50	05.00
6593 (Daily)	Nnd - Blr (Link)	22.10	22.50
6613 (Su)	Rjk - Cbe	09.40	09.50
6614 (Fri)	Cbe - Rjk	14.00	14.10
7225 (M,Th,Sa)	Vjd - Hbl (Amravati)	04.05	04.10
7226 (M,W,Sa)	Hbl - Vjd (Amravati)	17.05	17.10
7429 (Daily)	Hyd - Tpt (Rayalaseema)	01.40	02.10
7430 (Daily)	Tpt - Hyd (Rayalaseema)	01.00	02.45
7603 (Daily)	Kch - PNm	03.30	03.45
7604 (Daily)	Ypr - Kch	22.00	22.15

Train No.	Train Name	Arr.	Dep.
8463 (Daily)	Bbn - Blr	04.30	04.45
8464 (Daily)	Blr - Bbn	20.15	20.30
1028 (Daily)	Chn - Dud Mumbai Mail	08.05	08.25
1027 (Daily)	Mmb - Chn Chennai Mail	18.00	18.15
2736 (M,W,F)	Ypr - Sec	01.55	02.00
2735 Tu,Th,Su	Sec - Ypr	01.20	01.25
2975 Th, Sa	Mys - Jpr	19.15	19.30
2976 (M,W)	Jpr - Mys	06.25	06.40
6351 Tu, Sa	Mmb - Ngc	03.50	03.55
6352 (Th, Su)	Ngc - Mmb	03.45	03.50
6381 (Daily)	Mmb - Knk	07.45	07.50
6382 (Daily)	Knk - Mmb	10.30	10.50
8047 (M,Tu,Th,Sa)	Hwr - Vas (Amaravathy)	04.05	04.10
8048 (Tu,Th,F,Su)	Vas - Hwr	17.05	17.10

Vishakapatnam

Train No.	Train Name	Arr.	Dep.	Train No.	Train Name	Arr.	Dep.
1019 (Daily)	Mmb - Bbn (Konark)	20.55	21.15	2842 (Daily)	Chn - Hwr (Coromandal)	22.00	22.20
1020 (Daily)	Bbn - Mmb (Konark)	22.30	22.50	3351 (Daily)	Dbd - Alp	10.05	10.25
2659 (F)	Chn - Vsk	11.05	-	3352 (Daily)	Alp - Dbd	15.15	15.35
2660 (F)	Vsk - Chn	-	19.30	5227 (W)	Ypr - Mzr	23.15	23.35
2663 (Th,Su)	Hwr - Trc	05.50	06.35	5228 (M)	Mzr - Ypr	14.20	14.40
2665 (M)	Hwr - Knk	05.50	06.35	5629 (M)	Chn - Gwt	11.45	12.05
2835 (Tu,Su)	Hta - Ypr	09.45	10.05	5630 (F)	Gwt - Chn	05.50	06.35
2507 (Tu)	Enk - Gwt	23.15	23.35	5929 (Th)	Chn - Dgh	11.45	12.05
2703 (Daily)	Hwr - Sec (Falaknuma)	21.20	21.40	5930 (Su)	Dgh - Chn	05.50	06.35
2704 (Daily)	Sec - Hwr (Falaknuma)	03.30	03.50	6309 (M,Tu)	Enk - Ptn	19.30	19.50
2717 (Daily)	Vsk - Vjd (Ratnachal)	-	12.30	6310 (Th,F)	Ptn - Enk	14.20	14.40
2718 (Daily)	Vjd - Vsk (Ratnachal)	12.05	-	6323 (Th,Sa)	Tvm - Hwr	23.15	23.35
2803 (M, F)	Vsk - HNm (Swarna Jayanti)	-	08.30	6324 (Tu,Su)	Hwr - Tvm	14.20	14.40
2804 (W, Su)	HNm - Vsk (Swarna Jayanti)	17.25	-	7015 (Daily)	Bbn - Sec (Vishakha)	16.15	16.35
2805 (Daily)	Vsk - Vjd (Janmabhoomi)	-	06.00	7016 (Daily)	Sec - Bbn (Vishakha)	07.15	07.35
2806 (Daily)	Vjd - Vsk (Janmabhoomi)	19.40	-	7239 (Daily)	Gnt - Vsk (Simhadri)	17.50	-
2829 (F)	Chn - Bbn	10.25	10.45	7240 (Daily)	Vsk - Gnt (Simhadri)	-	07.10
2830 (Th)	Bbn - Chn	19.10	19.30	7479 (Ex.Tu,Sa)	Hwr - Tpt	22.50	23.15
2841 (Daily)	Hwr - Chn (Coromandal)	04.20	04.40	7480 (Ex.Su,Th)	Tpt - Hwr	04.40	05.00

Train No.	Train Name	Arr.	Dep.
7487 (Daily)	Tpt - Vsk (Thirumala)	10.55	-
7488 (Daily)	Vsk - Tpt (Thirumala)	-	13.50
8401 (Su)	Pri - Oka	17.25	17.45
8402 (W)	Oka - Pri	02.00	02.20

Vijayawada

Train No.	Train Name	Arr.	Dep.
1019 (Daily)	Mmb - Bbn	14.00	14.20
1020 (Daily)	Bbn - Mmb	05.00	05.20
1405 (Th,Su)	Mmd - Kkd	15.50	16.10
1406 (W, Sa)	Kkd - Mmd	10.10	10.35
2077 (Ex. Tu)	Chn - Vjd (Jan Shatabdi)	13.35	-
2078 (Ex. Tu)	Vjd - Chn (Jan Shatabdi)	-	14.35
2433 (Su, F)	Chn - HNm (Rajdhani)	11.55	12.05
2434 (W,F)	HNm - Chn (Rajdhani)	14.20	14.30
2615 (Daily)	Chn - Del (Grand Trunk)	02.00	02.10
2616 (Daily)	Del - Chn (Grand Trunk)	23.15	23.25
2621 (Daily)	Chn - Del (Tamil Nadu)	04.15	04.25
2622 (Daily)	Del - Chn (Tamil Nadu)	00.15	00.25
2625 (Daily)	Tvm - Del (Kerala Exp.)	10.05	10.20
2626 (Daily)	Del - Tvm (Kerala Exp.)	14.45	15.00
2641 (W)	Knk - HNm (Thirukkural Exp.)	15.55	16.10
2642 (Sa)	HNm - Knk (Thirukkural Exp.)	10.35	10.50
2643 (Tu)	Tvm - HNm	14.20	14.40
2644 (F)	HNm - Tvm	11.00	11.15
2645 (Sa)	Enk - HNm	14.20	15.40
2646 (Tu)	HNm - Enk	11.00	11.15
2655 (Daily)	Ahm - Chn (Navjivan)	08.45	09.00
2656 (Daily)	Chn - Ahm (Navjivan)	16.35	16.50
2703 (Daily)	Hwr - Sec (Falaknuma)	03.25	03.40
2704 (Daily)	Sec - Hwr (Falaknuma)	21.25	21.40
2705 (Daily)	Vjd - Sec (Intercity)	15.50	16.00
2706 (Daily)	Sec - Vjd (Intercity)	13.30	13.35
2711 (Daily)	Vjd - Chn (Pinakini)	-	06.00
2712 (Daily)	Chn - Vjd (Pinakini)	21.10	-
2713 (Daily)	Vjd - Sec (Satavahana)	-	06.10
2714 (Daily)	Sec - Vjd (Satavahana)	21.50	-
2717 (Daily)	Vsk - Vjd (Ratnachal)	18.20	-

Train No.	Train Name	Arr.	Dep.
2718 (Daily)	Vjd - Vsk (Ratnachal)	-	06.20
2759 (Daily)	Chn - Hyd (Charminar)	01.15	01.25
2760 (Daily)	Hyd - Chn (Charminar)	01.00	01.10
2763 (Ex.Tu,Th)	Tpt - Sec (Padmavathi)	23.25	23.35
2764 (Ex.Tu,Th)	Sec - Tpt (Padmavathi)	00.30	00.40
2803 (M, F)	Vsk - HNm (Swarna Jayanti)	14.20	14.40
2804 (W, Su)	HNm - Vsk (Swarna Jayanti)	11.05	11.25
2805 (Daily)	Vsk - Sec (Janmabhoomi)	11.45	11.50
2806 (Daily)	Sec - Vsk (Janmabhoomi)	13.30	13.40
2841 (Daily)	Hwr - Chn (Coromandal)	10.20	10.35
2842 (Daily)	Chn - Hwr (Coromandal)	15.35	15.50
2967 (Tu,Su)	Chn - Jpr	00.20	00.30
2968 (F,Su)	Jpr - Chn	02.20	02.30
3351 (Daily)	Dbd - Alp	18.10	18.40
3352 (Daily)	Alp - Dbd	07.10	07.30
5227 (W)	Ypr - Mzr	16.45	17.00
5228 (M)	Mzr - Ypr	20.40	20.55
5629 (M)	Chn - Gwt	05.30	05.40
5630 (F)	Gwt - Chn	12.25	12.40

Train No.	Train Name	Arr.	Dep.
5929 (F)	Chn - Dgh	05.30	05.40
5930 (W)	Dgh - Chn	12.25	12.40
6031 (W,Th,Su)	Chn - Jmt (Andaman Exp.)	14.30	14.50
6032 (Tu,F,Sa)	Jmt - Chn (Andaman Exp.)	00.40	01.00
6093 (Tu, Sa)	Chn - Lkn	14.30	14.50
6094 (M,Th)	Lkn - Chn	00.40	01.00
6125 (Sa)	Chn - Jdp	22.05	22.15
6126 (M)	Jdp - Chn	09.45	09.55
6309 (M,Tu)	Enk - Ptn	13.05	13.20
6310 (Th,F)	Ptn - Enk	20.40	20.55
6317 (F)	Knk - Jmt (Himsagar Exp.)	15.30	15.45
6318 (M)	Jmt - Knk (Himsagar Exp.)	19.05	19.20
6323 (Th,Sa)	Tvm - Hwr	16.45	17.00
6324 (Tu,Su)	Hwr - Tvm	20.40	20.55
6325 (M)	Idr - Tvm (Ahilyanagari Exp.)	16.10	16.25
6326 (Su)	Tvm - Idr (Ahilyanagari Exp.)	06.05	06.20
6327 (Th, Su)	Blp - Tvm	16.10	16.25
6328 (M,Th)	Tvm - Blp	06.05	06.20
6359 (Sa)	Enk - RNT	20.10	20.25

Train No.	Train Name	Arr.	Dep.
6360 (Tu)	RNT - Enk	02.50	03.00
6687 (M)	Mng/Mdr - Jmt (Navyug)	15.30	15.45
6688 (Th)	Jmt - Mng/Mdr (Navyug)	19.05	19.20
7015 (Daily)	Bbn - Sec (Visakha)	00.35	00.45
7016 (Daily)	Sec - Bbn (Visakha)	22.50	23.00
7049 (Daily)	Mch - Sec	21.55	22.20
7050 (Daily)	Sec - Mch	04.50	05.05
7201 (Daily)	Gnt - Sec (Golconda)	06.45	06.55
7202 (Daily)	Sec - Gnt (Golconda)	19.50	20.05
7203 (Su)	Bvr - Kkd	16.55	17.15
7204 (Su)	Kkd - Bvr	07.45	08.05
7209 (Daily)	Blr - Kkd (Sheshadri Exp.)	02.45	03.05
7210 (Daily)	Kkd - Blr (Sheshadri Exp.)	22.50	23.05
7225 (Daily)	Vjd - Hbl (Amravati)	-	18.55
7226 (M,W,Sa)	Lnd - Vjd (Amravati)	02.50	-
7239 (Daily)	Gnt - Vsk (Simhadri)	09.00	09.30
7240 (Daily)	Vsk - Gnt (Simhadri)	14.10	14.20
7255 (Daily)	Nrs - Hyd	22.20	22.35
7256 (Daily)	Hyd - Nrs	04.25	04.40

Train No.	Train Name	Arr.	Dep.
7405 (Daily)	Tpt - Hyd (Krishna)	13.15	13.30
7406 (Daily)	Hyd - Tpt (Krishna)	12.55	13.15
7479 (Ex.Tu,Sa)	Hwr - Tpt	08.00	08.20
7480 (Ex.Th,Su)	Tpt - Hwr	18.30	18.50
7487 (Daily)	Tpt - Vsk (Thirumala)	03.20	03.30
7488 (Daily)	Vsk - Tpt (Thirumala)	21.00	21.15
8401 (Su)	Pri - Oka	00.01	00.20
8402 (W)	Oka - Pri	19.05	19.25
2864 (Daily)	Ypr - Hwr	09.25	09.40
2863 (Daily)	Hwr - Ypr	16.45	17.00
2507 (Tu)	Enk - Hwr	16.45	17.00
2508 (F)	Gwt - Enk	21.40	21.55
2509 (W,Th,F)	Blr - Gwt	13.05	13.20
2510 (M,Tu,Su)	Gwt - Blr	21.40	21.55
2659 (Su)	Ngc - Slm (Gurudev)	16.00	16.20
2660 (W)	Slm - Ngc	20.40	20.55
2663 (Th,Su)	Hwr - Trc	12.25	12.40
2664 (Tu,F)	Trc - Hwr	05.30	05.40
2665 (M)	Hwr - Knk	12.25	12.40

Train No.	Train Name	Arr.	Dep.	Train No.	Train Name	Arr.	Dep.
2666 (Sa)	Knk - Hwr	05.30	05.40	2829 (F)	Chn - Bbn	04.00	04.10
2727 (Daily)	Vsk - Hyd (Godavari)	23.40	23.55	2830 (Th)	Bbn - Chn	01.25	01.35
2728 (Daily)	Hyd - Vsk	23.05	23.20	2839 (Daily)	Hwr - Chn	20.30	20.45
2516 (W)	Gwt - Tvm	21.40	21.55	2840 (Daily)	Chn - Hwr (Howrah Mail)	06.20	06.35
2515 (Su)	Tvm - Gwt	13.05	13.20	2846 (Tu)	Ypr - Bbn	21.35	21.55
2511 (Th,F,Su)	Gkp - Tvm (Rapti Sagar)	16.10	16.25	2845 (Su)	Bbn - Ypr	20.40	20.55
2512 (Tu,W,Su)	Tvm - Gkp	06.05	06.20	2897 (W)	Pdy - Bbn	05.30	05.40
2514 (Th)	Gwt - Sec	21.40	22.00	2898 (Tu)	Bbn - Pdy	01.25	01.35
2513 (Su)	Sec - Gwt	13.05	13.20	2970 (Tu)	Jpr - Cbe	02.20	02.30
2737 (Daily)	Kkd - Sec	00.20	00.35	2969 (F)	Cbe - Jpr	00.20	00.30
2738 (Daily)	Sec - Kkd	03.00	03.15	8645 (Daily)	Hwr - Hyd (East Coast)	11.00	11.20
				8646 (Daily)	Hyd - Hwr	16.30	16.50

Rajahmundry

Train No.	Train Name	Arr.	Dep.	Train No.	Train Name	Arr.	Dep.
1019 (Daily)	Mmb - Bbn	16.39	16.41	2704 (Daily)	Sec - Hwr (Falaknuma)	21.25	21.40
1020 (Daily)	Bbn - Mmb	01.48	01.50	2717 (Daily)	Vsk - Vjd (Ratnachal)	15.29	15.31
1405 (F, M)	Mmd - Kkd	18.30	18.32	2718 (Daily)	Vjd - Vsk (Ratnachal)	08.39	08.40
1406 (W, Sa)	Kkd - Mmd	07.13	07.15	2803 (M,F)	Vsk - HNm (Swarna Jayanthi Exp.)	11.18	11.20
2703 (Daily)	Hwr - Sec (Falaknuma)	00.27	00.29	2804 (W,Su)	HNm - Vsk (Swarna Jayanthi Exp.)	13.37	13.39

Train No.	Train Name	Arr.	Dep.
2805 (Daily)	Vsk - Vjd (Janmabhoomi)	08.58	09.00
2806 (Daily)	Vjd - Vsk (Janmabhoomi)	15.54	15.56
2841 (Daily)	Hwr - Chn (Coromandal)	07.27	07.29
2842 (Daily)	Chn - Hwr (Coromandal)	17.58	18.05
3351 (Daily)	Dbd - Alp	14.11	14.16
3352 (Daily)	Alp - Dbd	10.10	10.15
5227 (W)	Ypr - Mzr	19.08	19.13
5228 (M)	Mzr - Ypr	17.48	17.50
5629 (M)	Chn - Gwt	07.52	07.54
5630 (F)	Gwt - Chn	09.29	09.31
5929 (Th)	Chn - Dgh	07.52	07.54
5930 (Su)	Dgh - Chn	09.29	09.31
6309 (M,Tu)	Enk - Ptn	15.28	15.30
6310 (Th,F)	Ptn - Enk	17.48	17.50
6323 (Th,Sa)	Tvm - Hwr	19.08	19.13
6324 (Tu,Su)	Hwr - Tvm	17.48	17.50
7209 (Daily)	Blr - Kkd (Sheshadri)	07.23	07.25
7210 (Daily)	Kkd - Blr (Sheshadri)	18.35	18.40
7015 (Daily)	Bbn - Sec (Visakha)	19.50	20.05

Train No.	Train Name	Arr.	Dep.
7016 (Daily)	Sec - Bbn (Visakha)	03.00	03.20
7239 (Daily)	Gnt - Vsk (Simhadri)	13.15	13.20
7240 (Daily)	Vsk - Gnt (Simhadri)	10.35	10.40
7479 (Ex.Tu,Sa)	Hwr - Tpt	02.50	03.10
7480 (Ex.Th,Su)	Tpt - Hwr	23.50	00.25
7487 (Daily)	Tpt - Vsk (Thirumala)	06.02	06.07
7488 (Daily)	Vsk - Tpt	17.13	17.18
8401 (Su)	Pri - Oka	20.55	21.00
8402 (W)	Oka - Pri	21.37	21.39
2508 (F)	Gwt - Enk	18.53	18.55
2507 (Tu)	Enk - Gwt	19.08	19.13
2510 (M,Tu,Su)	Gwt - Blr	18.53	18.55
2509 (W,Th,F)	Blr - Gwt	15.28	15.30
2516 (W)	Gwt - Tvm	18.53	18.55
2515 (Su)	Tvm - Gwt	15.28	15.30
2660 (W)	Slm - Ngc (Gurudev)	17.48	17.50
2659 (Su)	Ngc - Slm	18.40	18.45
2664 (Tu,F)	Trc - Hwr	07.52	07.54
2665 (M)	Hwr - Trc	09.29	09.31

Train No.	Train Name	Arr.	Dep.
2666 (Sa)	Knk - Hwr	07.52	07.54
2738 (Daily)	Sec - Kkd	05.38	05.40
2737 (Daily)	Kkd - Sec	21.34	21.39
2829 (F)	Chn - Bbn	06.26	06.28
2830 (Th)	Bbn - Chn	22.24	22.26
2839 (Daily)	Hwr - Chn Hwh-Mas Mail	17.28	17.33
2840 (Daily)	Chn - Hwr	09.09	09.14
2861 (Daily)	Vsk - HNm Link Dakshin	18.14	18.16
2864 (Daily)	Ypr - Hwr	11.55	12.00
2863 (Daily)	Hwr - Ypr	13.53	13.55
2846 (Tu)	Ypr - Bbn	00.12	00.14
2845 (Su)	Bbn - Ypr	17.48	17.50

Train No.	Train Name	Arr.	Dep.
2889 (F)	Tata - Ypr	12.53	12.55
2890 (M)	Ypr - Tata	00.12	00.14
2897 (W)	Pdy - Bbn	07.52	07.54
2898 (Tu)	Bbn - Pdy	22.24	22.26
7205 (Tu)	Mmd - Kkd	18.30	18.32
7206 (M)	Kkd - Mmd	07.12	07.14
7643 (Daily)	Chn - Kkd (Circar)	08.05	08.10
7644 (Daily)	Kkd - Chn	15.58	16.03
8048 (Tu,Th,F,Su)	Vas - Kch	05.12	05.14
8047 (M,Tu,Th,Sa)	Hwr - Vas	15.48	15.50
8645 (Daily)	Hwr - Hyd (East Coast)	07.42	07.44
8646 (Daily)	Hyd - Hwr	19.24	19.29

SITE VIEW

Annavaram Temple: A hill-top temple on the banks of River Pampa. Presiding deity - Lord Veeravenkata Sathyanarayana Swamy. Important festivals - Bhishma Ekadasi, Kalyanotsavam. Distance from state capital - 498 k.m.

Penukonda Lord: A divine glimpse of the Lord at Penukonda, a hill resort of 934 m altitude, near Horsley Hill. Penukonda is also noted for its ancient ruins and a fort.

Charminar: This excellent piece of architecture, in the heart of the state capital, belongs to the 16th century. Built by Qutub-Shah it has four imposing minarets and a roof-top Mosque. This elegant edifice quite justifiably adorns many a portraits, wall hangers etc. which form a part of modern interior decoration. Each of its minarets measures to a height of 53 metres.

Warangal Nandhi: This Holy Bull-Mount of Lord Siva is housed in the triple-shrined temple complex, of which one is seen in the picture below. This black beautiful basalt image has been sculpted out of a single stone.

Ocean Park: Offers thrill and frill with a variety of pleasure rides. The restaurants in here offer multi-cuisine delicacies.

Warangal Temple: Built during the Chalukyan era. Fine architecture can be seen all over. The temple complex houses three shrines, one each dedicated to Lords Siva, Vishnu and Surya, the Sun God.

Osmania University: Comprises various colleges, research centres and departments. Offers Hostel facilities, canteens and playgrounds. Runs a separate college for women. Medium of instruction - Urdu. Houses a botanical garden on the campus. The structure - an elegant outcome of a combination of Ajantha, Arabian and Persian styles.

Birla Planetarium: Built with Japanese collaboration in 1985. Incorporates state-of-the-art equipment. The science museum on the campus offers copious entertainment. Situated opposite Naobat Hill, the planetarium and the museum receive hordes of visitors.

Bronze Image: Seen in the picture is the bronze image of Lord Nataraja (The Cosmic Dancer) a variation of Lord Siva. The intricate workmanship exposes the prowess of the craftsmen.

Lumbini Park: One of the chief attractions, this park is relatively a new addition on the banks of Hussain Sagar lake. It has interesting features such as the musical fountain. It remains open to visitors from 9.00 to 21.00 hrs. and closed on Mondays.

Cave Architecture: Seen in the picture is a beautifully carved image of Lord Krishna playing His divine Flute - a fine example of the cave architecture of ancient Andhra.

Salar Jung Museum: Salar Jung III after whom the museum is named was a voracious collector of antique objects par excellence. The museum houses a panoply of fabulous articles of arts and paintings. Japanese silk paintings, European paintings, handwritten Quran and a lot more can be seen.

Golconda Fort: An ancient citadel now in ruins. Situated on a secluded hill - 400 ft. above the surrounding plain. Contains 87 bastions. Outer walls - 5 m to 10 m thick; 15 m to 18 m high. The fort has 8 huge gates.